NYSTCE®

Literacy

Practice Questions

DEAR FUTURE EXAM SUCCESS STORY

First of all, **THANK YOU** for purchasing Mometrix study materials!

Second, congratulations! You are one of the few determined test-takers who are committed to doing whatever it takes to excel on your exam. **You have come to the right place.** We developed these practice tests with one goal in mind: to deliver you the best possible approximation of the questions you will see on test day.

Standardized testing is one of the biggest obstacles on your road to success, which only increases the importance of doing well in the high-pressure, high-stakes environment of test day. Your results on this test could have a significant impact on your future, and these practice tests will give you the repetitions you need to build your familiarity and confidence with the test content and format to help you achieve your full potential on test day.

Your success is our success

We would love to hear from you! If you would like to share the story of your exam success or if you have any questions or comments in regard to our products, please contact us at **800-673-8175** or **support@mometrix.com**.

Thanks again for your business and we wish you continued success!

Sincerely,
The Mometrix Test Preparation Team

TABLE OF CONTENTS

Practice Test #1

1. What is correct about evidence-based instructional strategies to use with ELL students?

a. Asking ELL students to explain and/or retell what teachers said to classmates is useful.
b. To get ELLs to concentrate on language, teachers should avoid incorporating visual aids.
c. Teachers should not "talk down" to ELLs by presenting abstract ideas in concrete forms.
d. Teachers may have ELLs signal when they don't understand, but they should not elaborate verbally.

2. Which of these is an indication that a child has problems with reading comprehension?

a. The child wonders about why the characters in a story did some things.
b. The child can tell how a story they read ended, but cannot explain why.
c. The child makes predictions about what will happen next in a narrative.
d. The child associates things in the reading with things in their own life.

3. In a rubric for scoring oral English language proficiency in English language learners (ELLs), which of these would most reflect a criterion at the highest proficiency level?

a. Being able to repeat English words and phrases
b. Being able to name concrete objects upon sight
c. Being able to participate in classroom discussions
d. Being able to communicate well in social contexts

4. Of the following, which is most correct in regard to children matching voice to print?

a. It is not normal for a second grader to finger-point to words when reading.
b. Giving young children creative, fun pointers is wrong, as these are crutches.
c. Older student finger-pointing shows reading struggles and impedes fluency.
d. Using bookmarks/popsicle sticks sideways has no effect on finger-pointing.

5. Suppose a teacher is helping students categorize animals as carnivores, herbivores, and omnivores using an explanation in a biology text. Which of the following types of exercises will be of most help to students in identifying these categories and their definitions as explained in the text?

a. Summarizing
b. Cloze sentences
c. Creative extension
d. Term memorization

6. Which of the following would you expect children in grades K–2 to learn by being exposed to both fictional and nonfictional literature?

a. How to tell fiction from nonfiction
b. How to do research to find information
c. How to tell if a nonfiction writer is writing from a biased viewpoint
d. How to understand themes, theories, and settings

7. A teacher wants to determine a student's accuracy and reading rate in order to determine if a text is in the student's frustration, instructional, or independent reading level. Which of the following assessments should she use?

a. Authentic assessment task
b. Rubric
c. Guided reading observation
d. Running record

8. Concerning student self-monitoring strategies in reading, which statement is true?

a. If students do not comprehend something, they should identify what and locate it in the text.
b. Students should only employ self-monitoring techniques when working with texts they understand well.
c. Self-monitoring is generally considered ineffective for students who struggle with reading.
d. If students do not comprehend something, previewing text by looking ahead makes it worse.

9. Students in a fourth-grade classroom read a novel about Alicia, a character who moves from a farm to a big city and struggles with the resulting changes in her lifestyle. After reading and discussing the text together, the teacher asks students to make a text-to-self connection. Which student response demonstrates a text-to-self connection?

a. Alicia reminds me a lot of Jacob in the book we read last semester. His family moved across the globe, and he had to adapt to the cultural differences in his new home.
b. I saw a story on the news about a girl who moved to a big city, and she helped set up a community garden in her new neighborhood.
c. Last year, I had to attend a new school because my family bought a new house in the city. It was hard at first to make new friends because everyone else already knew each other.
d. This was one of my favorite books we read this year because Alicia learned to make the best out of a difficult situation.

10. A preschool teacher is reading aloud to his students using a big book. He wants to help his students understand that the print carries the meaning of the story. What can the teacher do to foster this understanding?

a. Show students where to start reading on each page
b. Point to the words while reading
c. Model the return sweep at the end of each line of text
d. Ask students what they see in the pictures

11. A struggling reader has difficulty comprehending vocabulary words when they are encountered in unfamiliar texts. She frequently uses a dictionary to look up the unknown words. While this helps her figure out the meanings of the words, it interrupts her fluency and affects comprehension. Her teacher, Mr. Palmer, would like to teach her other strategies she can use instead that will minimize the disruptions to her fluency and increase her comprehension. Which strategy would likely be most effective?

a. Quickly asking a classmate for the meanings of the words
b. Creating a list of the unknown words and looking them up later
c. Trying to determine the meanings of the words from context clues
d. Skipping over the words she does not know as long as the sentences make sense

12. Which of these best identifies what developing automatic word recognition improves for students?

a. Recall quality and organization, via fluency and comprehension
b. Reading automaticity and speed, irrespective of comprehension
c. Reading comprehension, irrespective of how reading is recalled
d. Recall accuracy, organization, and detail irrespective of fluency

13. According to literacy experts, what is true about student writing?

a. The primary purpose of student writing is expressing their ideas, thoughts, and emotions.
b. The primary purpose of student writing is persuading their readers to agree with and believe them.
c. Improving student reading skills improves their writing skills, but not the other way around.
d. Improving student writing skills as well as their reading skills improves their learning ability.

14. Which of the following relates primarily to how sounds are represented in a text?

a. Syntactic
b. Semantic
c. Graphophonic
d. Pragmatic

15. Practical instructional activities that develop student listening skills include which of the following?

a. Teaching students how to follow rather than give directions
b. Teaching students how to give rather than follow directions
c. Teaching students interpersonal communication skills
d. Teaching students to appreciate conversation, not oral literature

16. Students in a fourth-grade class are reading and analyzing a fictional book about a girl, Samantha, who finds a wallet in the parking lot of a store. Which student response best demonstrates a prediction made using text evidence?

a. I think the book is mostly about honesty because Samantha ultimately decided to return the money she found.
b. I think Samantha will return the money because that is what I would do in her situation.
c. I think the author wrote the book to teach readers about the importance of being honest.
d. I think Samantha will decide to return the money because this chapter ends with her thinking about the bills the owner may need to pay with the money inside.

17. When reading grade-level texts, a third-grade student struggles to recognize both new and familiar vocabulary words. The student reads slowly, and often has trouble deriving meaning from what he has read. Based upon this information, this student appears to have difficulty with which of the following skills?

a. Irregular sight word recognition
b. Prosody
c. Phonemic awareness
d. Automaticity

18. Which student is most likely to need referral to a reading specialist for assessment, special instruction, or intervention?

a. Annabel: a second-grade student who tends to skip over words or phrases when she reads, affecting her comprehension of the text.
b. Cliff: a kindergarten student who is already reading simple chapter books with his parents at home or in class.
c. Noelle: a first grader who avoids any activity in which she must read, both aloud or silently, preferring to ask an adult to read the text for her first.
d. Barrett: a third grader who often confuses the sounds of certain letters, such as /b/ and /d/ or /v/ and /u/.

19. In an oddity task to demonstrate student ability to identify words with the same and different initial, medial, and final phonemes in words, which of these asks students to identify words with the same medial consonant sound?

a. Identifying *pan* and *cat* from among *pan, top,* and *cat*
b. Identifying *lesson* and *missing* in *lesson, kitten, missing*
c. Identifying *feet* as different among *late, feet,* and *take*
d. Identifying *ten* and *man* from among *ten, sat,* and *man*

20. The most effective strategy for decoding irregular sight words is:

a. Segmenting sight words into syllables. Beginning readers are understandably nervous when encountering a long word that isn't familiar. Blocking off all but a single syllable at a time renders a word manageable and allows the reader a sense of control over the act of reading.
b. Word families. By grouping the sight word with similar words, patterns emerge.
c. A phonemic approach. When students understand the connection between individual words and their sounds, they will be able to sound out any sight word they encounter.
d. None; irregular sight words cannot be decoded. Readers must learn to recognize these as whole words on sight.

21. Joseph is reading a book with fictional characters who live in modern times but travel back to the American Revolution to fight with the colonial soldiers. This book contains elements of which two genres of fiction?

a. Folktales and realistic fiction
b. Fantasy and historical fiction
c. Fable and fantasy
d. Historical fiction and folktale

22. A teacher uses a mixture of whole-group and small-group reading instruction. Which of the following activities would be the best choice for a whole-group lesson rather than small-group or individualized instruction?

a. Practice applying specific phonics skills
b. Independent reading of unfamiliar texts
c. Analyzing character development after the teacher reads a novel aloud
d. Spelling patterns

23. When reading aloud to students, a kindergarten teacher makes sure to speak expressively by pausing at the end of each sentence, changing intonation, and correlating inflection with differences in punctuation within the text. In doing so, the teacher models which of the following?

a. The correct usage of academic language
b. Differences in writing styles of literary and informational texts
c. Interest and enthusiasm for reading
d. The relationship between English grammatical conventions in written and spoken language

24. During assessment, a young child is able to identify and differentiate typical English-language speech sounds. This best reflects which type of awareness?

a. Phonic
b. Phonetic
c. Phonemic
d. Alphabetic

25. When teachers assign students to small groups for collaborative writing, which of these applies?

a. Teachers should only set individual performance expectations for individual, not group work.
b. Teachers should expect student groups to self-manage, and not interfere by giving structure.
c. Classmates in collaborative groups should give each other positive feedback, not corrections.
d. Classmates in collaborative groups should give each other constructive and positive feedback.

26. In a paired reading strategy for identifying the main idea in informational text, two students silently read a selection. Then, taking two-column notes of main ideas and supporting details, they take turns with the following steps. Which choice sequences these steps in the correct order?

a. The pair develops main idea consensus, a student paraphrases the main idea, a student explains agreement or disagreement, they take turns finding supporting details
b. A student paraphrases the main idea, a student explains agreement or disagreement, the pair develops main idea consensus, they take turns finding supporting details
c. They take turns finding supporting details, a student explains agreement or disagreement, a student paraphrases the main idea, the pair develops main idea consensus
d. A student explains agreement or disagreement, they take turns finding supporting details, the pair develops main idea consensus, a student paraphrases the main idea

27. Among some of the critical components of good phonics lessons, which one is taught for the purpose of helping students to decode unfamiliar words?

a. Introducing sound-spellings
b. Blending phonemes into words
c. Discriminating phonemes in words
d. Reviewing to overlearn sound-spellings

28. Government-funded research has found which of the following about phonics instruction?

a. It is equally effective regardless of whether it is systematic and explicit or not.
b. It is more effective for children of certain socioeconomic levels than for others.
c. It is equally effective regardless of the age or grade levels when introduced.
d. It is more effective when students can understand and apply their learning.

29. Sixth-grade students are taking a standardized, criterion-referenced reading test. Part of the test involves answering comprehension questions based on reading passages. Some of the passages contain cultural references that some groups of students do not understand, causing them to miss multiple questions. This is an example of a testing concern in which area?

a. Validity
b. Reliability
c. Bias
d. Consistency

30. A fourth-grade teacher is planning to have students independently read a grade-level work of fictional literature. First, the teacher administers a diagnostic comprehension test and uses the results to select a small group of students that scored below grade level to work with the paraprofessional in the classroom. While in the group, students read independently, respond to discussion questions from the paraprofessional, and after reading, complete activities related to the text. This is an example of which of the following techniques for promoting reading comprehension?

a. Think-pair-share
b. Guided reading
c. Close reading
d. Contextual analysis

31. A first-grade teacher is planning instruction focused on the structural analysis of words to promote vocabulary acquisition and decoding skills. Which of the following strategies would be most effective in achieving this?

a. Using rhymes and songs to promote phonemic awareness
b. Having the class participate in a choral reading of a familiar text
c. Creating a word-building game in which students construct vocabulary from a set of root words and affixes
d. Holding a reader's theater in which students act out dialogue from a story

32. A high school English teacher asked the students to read a magazine article about the Uffizi Gallery in Florence, Italy, and its collection of Italian Renaissance paintings. The teacher advised the students to annotate the text with comments and questions. Later the students would discuss their respective annotations. What does Jason's comment indicate about what he learned?

Jason's annotation: The Italian Renaissance produced some of the world's greatest masterpieces from the thirteenth to the sixteenth centuries.

a. He understands the timeline of the historical period of the collection.
b. He knows about the content of the paintings in the collection.
c. He recognizes the names of the artists who did these paintings.
d. He knows about the architecture of this museum.

33. According to experts, which of the following is an accurate distinction regarding phonological awareness and phonemic awareness?

a. Phonological awareness distinguishes speech sounds from meanings.
b. There is no real distinction; they are synonyms used interchangeably.
c. Phonological awareness involves sounds, phonemic involves speech.
d. Phonemic awareness is the less sophisticated level between the two.

34. Which of the following is most accurate about the benefits of various levels of phonological awareness instruction to the development of reading skills?

a. Instruction in rhyming, onsets, and rimes appears most directly beneficial to reading development.
b. Instruction in simpler phonology skills can aid teaching more complex ones and reading development.
c. Instruction that integrates blending and segmenting appears most beneficial to reading development.
d. Instruction that integrates deleting and substituting appears most beneficial to reading development.

35. A fourth-grade teacher gives students a character chart to fill out while reading a fictional text. Students are instructed to record traits of the main character as they read. One student, Daniel, turns in a map that lists the following traits: short, has blond hair, has freckles, is a girl. Which strategy would be an appropriate next step for the teacher to focus on?

a. Analyzing character development from the beginning of the story to the end
b. Identifying the character as a protagonist or antagonist
c. Differentiating between internal and external character traits
d. Comparing and contrasting the character with a character from another book by the same author

36. A second-grade teacher is planning a lesson focused on identifying the main idea of an informational text. After carefully researching, the teacher chooses a developmentally appropriate multi-paragraph online article about the impacts of environmental changes. For new vocabulary words, the teacher plans to scaffold definitions and provide several examples for additional clarification. In doing so, this teacher demonstrates knowledge of which of the following?

a. Evidence-based strategies for selecting instructional materials that are aligned with state learning standards and appropriate for meeting students' needs in language and literacy
b. Differentiating instruction to accommodate a variety of skills and ability levels in literacy
c. Methods for developing phonological awareness in young children
d. Strategies for emphasizing the connection between spoken and written language

Refer to the following for question 37.

A seventh-grade teacher asks the reading teacher to suggest a lesson that students will find simultaneously challenging and fun. The reading teacher suggests the class read fairy tales from both Hans Christian Anderson and the Brothers Grimm and have a rapid-paced, energetic discussion about the many similarities and differences between the two while the teacher lists them on the board.

37. The primary benefit of this exercise is that it promotes students':

a. Vocabulary
b. Comprehension
c. Fluency
d. Word identification

38. Which of the following activities best demonstrates a phonics activity?

a. Sorting rhyming words
b. Playing alphabet bingo and covering a letter when the teacher says its name
c. Matching picture cards to the consonant blends they begin with
d. Listening to a fictional story read aloud by the teacher and identifying the setting

39. A third-grade student has difficulties with decoding and struggles to read grade-level texts independently. Which statement is likely to be true based on this information?

a. The student will benefit from additional implicit phonics instruction.
b. The student will also struggle with phonological awareness.
c. The student will also struggle with fluency and comprehension.
d. The student likely has a language processing disorder and requires further evaluation.

40. Which of these is accurate about instruction that supports independent, reflective student reading?

a. Students typically write in reader response journals after both sustained silent and independent reading.
b. Student journals enable teachers to monitor reading, check comprehension, discuss, and suggest books.
c. Students typically can write in reader response journals without any modeling, prompting, or references.
d. Students should be advised to achieve a balance of 50 percent reading and 50 percent writing.

41. Olivia, a first-grade student, has a reading intervention plan to improve her decoding of CVCe words. In addition to working with the teacher in a small group each day, Olivia's teacher gives her 10 new CVCe words to decode each Friday. The number of words read correctly is recorded on a graph, and the teacher notes any improvement made from the previous weeks. Which type of assessment is the teacher demonstrating?

a. Progress monitoring
b. Screening assessment
c. Summative assessment
d. Norm-referenced assessment

42. A sentence in a book states, "It is fun to play checkers." Which of the following examples demonstrates an error related to meaning, if stated by a student reading the text?

a. It is fun playing checkers.
b. It is fun to play chess.
c. It is fun to play games.
d. It is fun to play checkers with friends.

43. Prior to launching a sixth-grade genre study on historical fiction, Mrs. Perez plans to create a list of vocabulary words to explicitly teach to her students. She wants to select tier-two words that will best contribute to students' overall language development and allow them to transfer their knowledge to other reading experiences. Which words fit these criteria?

a. Challenging but common vocabulary words that carry a lot of meaning
b. High-frequency, concrete nouns
c. Domain-specific words found in students' social studies textbooks
d. Student-selected words related to their interests within the genre

44. A teacher introduces a new book about water conservation to students and says, "As you read this book, locate three ways you can conserve water at home." What is her primary reason for this statement?

a. To encourage students to consider the author's purpose
b. To help students set a purpose for reading
c. To activate students' prior knowledge
d. To encourage students to make text-to-text connections

45. A first-grade teacher works with students of varying levels of literacy skill development. Which of the following strategies would likely best address these students' individual learning needs to build fluency and promote reading comprehension skills?

a. Homogenous flexible grouping with leveled texts
b. Scheduling daily class read-aloud time
c. Creating a print-rich environment
d. Providing struggling students with individualized instruction

46. A fifth-grade teacher is helping his students analyze how varied sentence structure contributes to the tone and mood of a text. Which of the following sentences should he use if he wants to model a complex sentence?

a. Michael ate pancakes for breakfast.
b. Michael ate breakfast and brushed his teeth.
c. Before going to school, Michael brushed his teeth.
d. Michael ate breakfast, and he brushed his teeth.

47. According to recent research findings, diagnosed reading difficulties such as dyslexia are primarily ______ in origin.

a. Neurological and developmental
b. Environmental and ecological
c. Neurological and environmental
d. Developmental and environmental

48. Among the following reasons that readers must deduce informational author purposes and motivations for writing, which is most important for identifying purposes an author may have had but did not state in the text?

a. Determining an author's purpose enables readers to know what to expect from the text.
b. Discovering the author's motivation for writing allows readers to read for relevant details.
c. Knowing author motivation and purpose enables critical reader evaluation of author and text.
d. When authors define purposes contradicting some text, they may have hidden agendas.

49. Which of the following linguistic domains does NOT play a role in decoding unfamiliar words when reading?

a. Syntactic
b. Semantic
c. Graphophonic
d. Pragmatic

50. A kindergarten student has difficulty enunciating words, which is impacting her ability to communicate clearly and intelligibly. For example, she often mumbles words and pronounces both the letters "r" and "l" as "w". Which of the following interventions would be most effective in developing this student's speaking skills?

a. Pairing the student with another who can provide scaffolding during speaking activities
b. Reviewing the pronunciation of regular and irregular sight words
c. Providing the student with individualized instruction focused on letter and word sounds
d. Implementing assistive technology to alleviate the student's speech difficulties

51. Which of the following instructional strategies would likely help students the most in understanding the difference between denotation and connotation and help them learn to identify the connotation of a word in context?

a. Providing example sentences in multiple choice questions asking for a word's connotation
b. Filling out a Venn diagram with sets of words that have connotations, denotations, or both
c. Assigning a reading where students identify and highlight words that have connotations
d. Giving word definitions and asking students to describe the feelings elicited by each definition

52. A teacher wants to help his students identify the types of nonfiction texts they are reading based on their text structures. Which keywords would students likely find in compare-and-contrast texts?

a. For example and for instance
b. Similarly and on the other hand
c. Because and as a result
d. First, next, and finally

53. Which of the following options would be the most effective way to modify a cloze reading passage for struggling readers to assist them with completing the task while still allowing them to practice the skill?

a. Providing the first few letters of each answer
b. Including a word bank
c. Having students work in pairs
d. Including no more than three omitted words

54. What should a young child NOT be able to identify during informal assessment of print concept awareness?

a. Where the teacher should start reading aloud
b. The title of the book
c. What a period means in a book
d. All of the words in the book

55. In which of the following genres of children's books does each book typically cover a single topic, such as birds, butterflies, reptiles, transportation, weather, etc.?

a. Children's fiction
b. Children's story books
c. Children's poetry books
d. Children's information books

56. A second-grade teacher is reading a student's journal entry and sees the following set of sentences:

"I lisened to a great story. Then my teacher asked a question, and I ansered it."

Based on these sentences, which skill would be most beneficial for the teacher to focus on with the student?

a. Consonant blends
b. Consonant digraphs
c. Silent letter spelling patterns
d. Subject/verb agreement

57. Of the following influences on student reading comprehension, which one is a psychological factor?

a. Attention
b. Perception
c. Motivation
d. Working memory

58. Which choice constitutes the best method for building conceptual vocabulary?

a. Using word webs to organize thinking about related terms
b. Previewing vocabulary words for upcoming units in other subjects such as science or social studies
c. Implementing a framework for introducing students to various concepts over time
d. Practicing sight words

59. A kindergarten teacher has created four literacy learning stations in the classroom, with each focused on a specific component of phonics instruction. Every week, students are assigned to work in a particular station based upon their level of skill development, and the teacher monitors progress using an observation checklist to determine which stations to assign for the following week. Implementing this strategy allows this teacher to do which of the following?

a. Provide hands-on learning opportunities
b. Allow for flexibility and student choice
c. Differentiate literacy instruction
d. Modify learning activities

60. On a continuum, which of these represents the most complex level of phonological awareness?

a. Segmenting words into their individual syllables and blending individual syllables into words
b. Phonemic awareness, i.e., understanding words consist of phonemes and manipulating these
c. Segmenting words into their onsets and rimes and blending onsets and rimes into full words
d. Segmenting sentences, i.e., understanding speech consists of separate words, and rhyming songs

61. Which of these accurately reflects research findings related to literary genre studies?

a. Research finds experience reading various genres unrelated to writing in various genres.
b. Research finds literary analysis requires applying different strategies and skills by genre.
c. Research finds analyzing different literary genres contributes to cognitive development.
d. Research finds deeper immersion in one to two genres more important than exposure to many.

62. Which statement is correct about how teachers can model appropriate listening and speaking behaviors for students?

a. Teachers can model these when they facilitate book discussions, not in everyday conversations.
b. Teachers can model these better when giving whole-class instruction rather than small-group teaching.
c. Teachers can model these more authentically in one-to-one conversations than in discussions of media.
d. Teachers can model these and support them by thinking aloud about specific content they teach.

63. Among effective reading strategies, which one involves recalling relevant past experience and existing knowledge to construct meaning from the new information in text that one reads?

a. Inferring
b. Activating
c. Questioning
d. Summarizing

64. In implementing a new school reading program, school leaders and leadership teams must rise to the challenge of managing teacher "domestication" of the new program—i.e., altering its design to do it their own way, which frequently decreases its effectiveness—when during its implementation?

a. During the third year of its implementation
b. During the first year of its implementation
c. During the second year of implementation
d. During the fourth year of implementation

65. Which of these sets of factors would most greatly affect a student's reading comprehension in class and on tests?

a. Oral language development, written language development and eating a healthy breakfast.
b. Word analysis skills, sight word knowledge and ability to monitor understanding.
c. Vocabulary development, sight word knowledge and reference skills.
d. Prior knowledge, good classroom participation and academic performance in other subjects.

66. Which instructional strategy would be most appropriate to assist a student with retention difficulties in analyzing the plot of a fictional text?

a. Providing the student with a story map
b. Having the student read the story twice before responding to questions
c. Playing an audio version of the story rather than having the student read a printed version
d. Asking the student to complete a KWL chart before and after reading

67. A student encounters a multisyllabic word. She's not sure if she's seen it before. What should she do first? What should she do next?

a. Locate familiar word parts, then locate the consonants
b. Locate the consonants, then locate the vowels
c. Locate the vowels, then locate familiar word parts
d. Look it up in the dictionary, then write down the meaning

68. Mr. Suarez teaches a preschool class containing students in the preliterate stage of writing. He wants to help his students understand the relationship between spoken and written words using a familiar topic, so he has planned an activity relating to the class's recent field trip to the apple orchard. Mr. Suarez will help the group record memories of their field trip in writing while they contribute ideas, and Mr. Suarez will read the writing back to students repeatedly throughout the week. Which activity would be most appropriate?

a. Shared writing
b. Independent writing
c. Interactive writing
d. Partner writing

69. A teacher gives students the following set of words: *compare, organism, predict, cell, habitat,* and *conclude*. Students are instructed to sort the words into two categories. What is the primary purpose of this activity?

a. Classifying words according to morphology
b. Recognizing common spelling patterns used to decode words
c. Differentiating between academic and content vocabulary
d. Grouping words with similar meanings

70. A second-grade teacher would like to promote students' ability to read independently and retell stories by recalling major details, such as the characters, plot, setting, and central message. Which of the following instructional resources would be most beneficial in achieving this?

a. Story maps that students can complete as they read
b. Comprehension questions that correspond with each story
c. Anticipation guides for students to complete prior to engaging in reading
d. Pretests to activate students' prior knowledge

71. Research has indicated that which of the following options is the best predictor of early reading success?

a. Phonemic awareness
b. Interest in reading
c. Concepts of print
d. Oral vocabulary

72. Which of these is NOT a pair of low-impact teacher interventions that prevent undesirable student behaviors from escalating?

a. Showing interest in student work and encouraging students in their endeavors
b. Showing awareness of student behaviors through physical proximity and touch
c. Embarrassing and punishing students in front of classmates to prevent rebellion
d. Reminding students of successful instances and modifying lesson presentations

73. What is one benefit of implicit phonics instruction?

a. It leads to stronger decoding skills.
b. Its progression from part to whole increases proficiency more quickly.
c. Research suggests it is the most effective approach to phonics instruction.
d. Phonics skills are taught in a meaningful context.

74. Which example best demonstrates the writing or drawing of *candy* typical of a child in the transitional stage of writing development?

a. 
b. Csce
c. Cande
d. Candy

75. In describing a literacy-rich learning environment for younger students, what is most correct?

a. Labeling everything in the classroom only distracts the attention of the youngest students.
b. Directions, calendars, signs, and schedules are organizational tools not supporting literacy.
c. Word and picture labels should be avoided for discriminating against the visually impaired.
d. Students experience lessons directly if they and teachers redo classrooms as themes or texts.

76. Which of these correctly represents findings about research-based vocabulary instruction?

a. Children need word repetition consisting of drills for vocabulary development.
b. Children need only be exposed to new words once or twice to remember them.
c. Children learn the vocabulary in texts best indirectly through simply reading them.
d. Children require direct instruction and word exposure in various contexts.

77. Liz, a third grader, is completing a reading assessment with her teacher. During the fluency component of the assessment, she reads a short passage aloud. Her teacher notes that Liz's reading rate is in the average range for her grade level, and she correctly decodes 95% of the words in the passage. However, Liz reads in a monotone voice and often forgets to pause before beginning new sentences. Which component of fluency should Liz's teacher target during small-group instruction?

a. Accuracy
b. Automaticity
c. Word recognition
d. Prosody

78. A kindergarten teacher uses color-coded letter cards to spell a word and asks students to read it aloud. The teacher then replaces one letter card with a different one, and asks students to identify the new word. For example, after spelling the word "cat," the teacher replaces the letter "c" with "b" and asks students to read the new word. This strategy is likely intended to teach which of the following skills?

a. Phoneme substitution
b. Alliteration
c. Identification of rhyming words
d. The alphabetic principle

79. While speaking to his friend, a fifth-grade student says, "Hey, you should read this book. It's awesome." Later, while presenting an oral book report in front of his class and teacher, he says, "This book is full of suspense. The author leaves you wondering if the main character will be rescued from the mountain before it is too late. I highly recommend you read it to find out if he is rescued in time." This example best demonstrates the role of what in language usage?

a. Social context
b. Cultural context
c. Contextual clues
d. Personal context

80. Which of the following statements is correct regarding the reader's process of identifying author purpose in informational text?

a. Stated purposes conflicting with other parts of the text may signal a hidden agenda.
b. Authors of informational text always state the most important purposes of the text.
c. The main or central idea of a text and the purpose of that text are the same thing.
d. Identifying unstated author purposes for texts offers no advantages to the readers.

81. The use of analogies is most appropriate for helping students achieve which instructional objective?

a. Analyzing common roots and affixes
b. Defining words
c. Identifying word origins
d. Recognizing the relationships between words

82. Which of these have researchers found about the relationship of family involvement in education to student outcomes?

a. Students with families involved in their learning get higher grades, take more advanced classes, have higher graduation rates, and are more likely to attend postsecondary education.
b. Students perform their best academically when their parents concentrate on adopting one specific major role in their learning, like participating in school events and activities.
c. Students whose families actively support their learning have better attendance and attitudes toward school, but do not demonstrate any better behavior while they are there.
d. Students from diverse backgrounds feel more comfortable in school as a result of school-family collaboration to bridge cultural gaps, but are not found to perform better academically.

83. To practice decoding skills, a first-grade teacher has students clap out each sound of multisyllabic words. Which of the following additional strategies would best promote the development of this skill for children in this age group?

a. Exposing students to new multisyllabic words in a variety of contexts
b. Having students cut and paste letters to form multisyllabic words
c. Using a semantic map to demonstrate the features of new multisyllabic words
d. Having students identify the prefixes and suffixes of multisyllabic words

84. A first-grade student struggles to decode words containing *oo* in their spellings because that vowel combination makes two common sounds. Which prompt would be most likely to assist the student with decoding these words when encountered in texts?

a. Look for parts of the word you already know.
b. Use visual clues to guess the word and make sure that your guess looks right.
c. Read the word both ways in the sentence to see which way makes sense.
d. Think of similar words you know that have the same spelling pattern.

85. Which of these is mainly a sign that a student has problems with reading comprehension?

a. The student has trouble recognizing words out of context.
b. The student reads laboriously, reading one word at a time.
c. The student has trouble separating the main idea from details.
d. The student has trouble relating a text to prior knowledge.

86. During informal assessment, which of these is the best example of print awareness in a young child?

a. The child can identify the front and the back of a book.
b. The child can identify all letters in the words in a book.
c. The child can identify words but not spaces in between.
d. The child can identify and read sentences with fluency.

87. A third-grade teacher has noticed that a student is having difficulty recognizing and spelling high-frequency sight words. In addition, when writing, he often skips words and writes letters backwards. Which of the following is the most appropriate response in this situation?

a. Provide the student with individualized instruction to develop his skills.
b. Pair the student with another that can provide scaffolding.
c. Implement response to intervention (RTI) services.
d. Refer the student for an initial evaluation with the special education department.

88. Which of the following strategies would best demonstrate to prekindergarten students the purpose and use of a printed book?

a. Taking a class trip to the school library
b. Asking students to bring in their favorite book from home
c. Modeling how to hold a book, turn pages, read from left to right, and pointing out key characteristics
d. Incorporating time for reading aloud into the school day

89. Educational researchers have found which of the following literary genres most appropriate for improving reading comprehension in public schools?

a. Novels
b. Poems
c. Short stories
d. Drama (plays)

90. Before reading a nonfiction book about habitats, students are given a list of statements about the content and asked if they agree or disagree with them. After reading, they return to the list and their initial responses and indicate if they still agree with their choices or if their thoughts have changed as a result of new information gained while reading. What type of tool does this example describe?

a. Storyboard
b. Anticipation guide
c. Concept map
d. Outline

Answer Key and Explanations for Test #1

1. A: Research finds one helpful instructional strategy for ELL student language acquisition is to have them explain and/or retell what the teacher just said to their classmates. This not only ensures their comprehension, but it also gives them practice analyzing the English they hear, restating/paraphrasing English, and communicating to others in spoken English. Teachers should incorporate visual aids: studies show supplementing verbal input visually helps ELLs understand concepts in subject content areas as they are learning a foreign language. Research finds that students cannot grasp abstract concepts as readily in a foreign language, so teachers should give them concrete objects, pictures, and the like to illustrate and demonstrate ideas as students gradually transition from concrete to abstract in a new language. Teachers can arrange for ELLs to signal when they don't understand; they also closely observe ELLs, and if they do not indicate or demonstrate understanding, they should elaborate by summarizing, paraphrasing, and giving synonyms.

2. B: If a child can repeat the factual elements of how a story ended, but cannot explain why this ending occurred, this may show that the child cannot reason about cause and effect, logic, and sequencing in the material s/he has read; and/or lacks the expressive language skills to explain. Wondering about characters' reasons for their actions (A) indicates comprehension, not its lack: readers with good comprehension will speculate about character motivations, and will also try to predict future events in a book (C) before reading of them. Relating reading matter to one's own life (D) and pre-existing knowledge also does not indicate comprehension problems, but rather good reading comprehension.

3. C: Being able to repeat English words and phrases (A) and name concrete objects on sight (B) are both examples of criteria at the lowest level of an oral ELP scoring rubric. Being able to communicate well in social contexts (D) is an example of a rubric criterion for an intermediate ELP level. At the highest level, the student would communicate *very* well, not only in social but also academic contexts. Being able to participate in classroom discussions (C) is an example of the highest ELP level.

4. C: Finger-pointing is normal for beginning readers, even into second grade (A); adults should not interfere with pointing. Giving young children "witch fingers," feathers, and other available, recycled, or homemade pointers is fine. These are not crutches (B); they are simply finger substitutes that are creative, fun, and keep book pages clean with younger readers. However, when older students finger-point, it can indicate reading struggles and interfere with reading fluency (C). Having students turn bookmarks or popsicle sticks sideways to mark each line of text helps them transition past finger-pointing (D).

5. B: Cloze sentences are sentences with certain words or phrases from a given text replaced with blanks. They allow students to fill in the blanks and thereby use a reasoning process to learn the meanings of terms. This type of activity would be the most effective of those listed in the other answer choices for helping students understand the text and the terms it presents, so choice B is correct. Summarizing may be helpful, but it would not target specific terms, as cloze sentences would, so choice A is incorrect. Creative extension would help in applying the concepts one they are learned, but it would not be possible until the concepts are learned, so choice C is incorrect. Rote memorization would not enable students to use reasoning, so it would not necessarily be an aid to understanding the text or the terms, so choice D is incorrect.

6. A: Telling fiction from nonfiction is a skill that children learn by following clues within the literature that point out whether the story is true or not. Young children are not yet ready to distinguish bias in an author's writing or understand themes and theories.

7. D: When completing a running record, a teacher records the number of words the student reads correctly out of the total number of words in the text. This is used to calculate the accuracy rate, which helps to determine if the text is at the student's frustration, instructional, or independent reading level. Authentic assessment tasks provide opportunities for students to complete reading and writing activities while solving real-world problems rather than opportunities to calculate the accuracy rate when reading a text. Rubrics are used to evaluate students' performances based on multiple criteria on assignments and assessments, but they are not used to calculate accuracy rate, either. Guided reading observations may help the teacher determine if a text is much too easy or much too difficult for a student to read independently, but without the running record, the exact accuracy rate cannot be determined.

8. A: One self-monitoring strategy to aid reading comprehension is for students to locate the problem by isolating what part of the text they do not understand, which words were difficult, and specifically what did not make sense to them. Another self-monitoring strategy for students is trying to paraphrase the text they had trouble understanding, which often helps. An additional strategy is to review the text for earlier instances of the same topic or information the student finds unclear to see if those shed light on the current instance. Another self-monitoring strategy is to preview the text to see if explanations, elaboration, illustrations or other graphics later in the text might clarify what students are currently reading. Self-monitoring techniques are important tools for those who struggle with reading, and they can be employed at all difficulty levels.

9. C: When students make text-to-self connections, they make connections between the texts and their own personal experiences. This student connects Alicia's experiences adjusting to a new situation to her own adjustment when moving to a new school. Choice A demonstrates a text-to-text connection, when students make connections between two or more different texts they have read. Choice B demonstrates a text-to-world connection, when students make connections between texts and events that have happened in the real world, but not to themselves personally. Choice D represents a student's reaction to the book rather than a connection between two or more things.

10. B: Pointing to each word as it is read aloud will help students understand the relationship between the printed and spoken word. They will begin to understand that the meaning of the story is contained in the text. Showing students where to begin reading on each page and how to complete a return sweep will help them track the text appropriately. Asking students what they see in the pictures encourages the use of the semantic cueing system.

11. C: Using context clues can help the reader determine the meanings of many unknown words quickly and also contribute to reading comprehension. Asking a classmate for the meanings of words may work in the short term, but it does not help the reader develop independent reading strategies, and there may not always be another person present while reading. Looking up the unknown words later may result in the student missing words that are critical to the meaning of the text, negatively affecting comprehension. Similarly, while skipping over the unknown words may result in sentences that appear to make sense, the missing words may play important roles in the meaning.

12. A: The more words a student can recognize automatically when reading, the more fluently he or she reads, with better comprehension; these in turn dramatically enhance the student's ability to recall the reading more accurately, with greater organization and detail. Fluency without understanding (B), understanding without fluency (C), and improved recall without or regardless of fluency (D) are hence incorrect.

13. D: Research into literacy development reveals that improvement in students' writing skills improves their overall learning ability, just as improvement in their reading skills also does. Expressing ideas, thoughts, and feelings (A) is *one* purpose of student writing, but not the only or main one. Another purpose is persuasion of the reader audience to agree with the writer's point of view and/or believe the writer's assertions—again, not the only or main purpose (B), but one of various purposes. Research also finds not only that improving student reading skills improves their writing, but *also* that, reciprocally, improving student writing skills improves their reading (C).

14. C: Graphophonic cues are based on the speech sounds in words and their alphabetic representations in print, so choice C is correct. Syntactic cues (A) are based on how words are arranged and ordered to create meaningful phrases, clauses and sentences. Semantic cues (B) are based on the meanings of morphemes and words and how they combine to create additional meanings. Pragmatic cues (D) are based on the readers' purposes for reading and their understanding of how textual structures function in the texts that they read.

15. C: Practical instructional activities that develop student listening skills (cf. Wolvin and Coakley, 1979) include teaching students both to follow and give directions, teaching them interpersonal communication skills, and teaching them to appreciate oral literature.

16. D: Choice D includes a prediction because the student tells what she thinks is going to happen in the story. She also includes text evidence by explaining how the clue at the end of the chapter influenced her prediction. Choice A shows the student describing the theme of the story. Choice B includes a prediction, but the student has supported it with a personal connection rather than using text evidence. Choice C shows the student's explanation of the author's purpose for writing the story.

17. D: Automaticity refers to one's ability to quickly recognize and understand written words. This skill is fundamental to the development of reading fluency, and is cultivated by frequent exposure to new vocabulary, printed words, and patterns of phonics. Students that struggle with automaticity typically have trouble recognizing written words, reading at a grade-level-appropriate pace, and comprehending what they have read. Difficulty with automaticity in reading may result from numerous factors, such as limited phonics knowledge or exposure to printed language, weak decoding skills, or a learning disability. As this skill is integral to language and literacy development, struggling students must receive necessary interventions and support.

18. D: Teachers will observe a variety of developmental arcs when teaching reading, since all students learn differently. It is very important to understand which instances are normal in the course of learning and which signal a learning difficulty. Barrett is still exhibiting confusion over certain letter-sounds, typically when the letters look similar. At his age, this difficulty could suggest that Barrett has an issue with reading that could be addressed by a reading specialist. The other three choices describe normal behaviors that are commonly exhibited by children when they are learning to read. Choice C, Noelle, may describe an instance in which a student is having a learning problem. However, the teacher will need more information about Noelle's reading skills besides her reluctance to read before making a determination about how to proceed.

19. B: Both words identified in this choice have the same medial consonant sound of /s/, whereas *kitten* has the medial consonant /t/. The two words identified in choice A have the same medial *vowel* sound. The one word identified in choice C has a different medial *vowel* sound than the other two. The two words identified in choice D have the same *final* consonant sound; the other word does not.

20. D: None; irregular sight words cannot generally be decoded. Readers must learn to recognize these as whole words on sight. They either have irregular spelling or do not follow typical phonic patterns, so an attempt at decoding may ultimately mislead the reader. Segmenting them into syllables or using a phonemic approach are ineffective strategies to aid a reader in recognizing a sight word because these approaches depend on rules a sight word doesn't follow. Word families group words that share common patterns of consonants and vowels. The spelling of those words is, therefore, regular because they follow a predictable pattern. Sight words that are irregular, do not follow a predictable pattern, and must be instantaneously recognized for writing fluency. Decoding is not useful.

21. B: This book contains elements of fantasy due to the time travel, and it contains elements of historical fiction with the characters' participation in the American Revolution. Choice A is incorrect because it is not a story passed down over time, so it is not a folktale. Additionally, while some portions of the story may seem realistic, the time traveling element makes it more fantasy than realistic fiction. Choice C is incorrect because the story doesn't focus on a moral or contain talking animals. Choice D is incorrect because it is not a folktale.

22. C: One of the challenges of large-group instruction is meeting the needs of diverse learners. Reading a novel aloud helps to make the content accessible to all learners. If students were to read it independently, as in choice B, the text would likely not be challenging enough for some readers and too difficult for others. Therefore, basing a comprehension lesson on a book that was read aloud assists all students with participating. While teachers sometimes introduce and practice phonics skills in large groups, students are likely to have differing skill levels in this area. Proficient first-grade readers, for example, may read consonant blends and digraphs with ease, which struggling readers may still be learning the alphabetic principle. Students in a classroom are also likely to have vastly different spelling skills, making the need for differentiation important.

23. D: Recognizing the characteristics and functions of English grammatical conventions is important for reading comprehension development. Further, modeling to students how these patterns apply to spoken language is necessary for fostering reading fluency and expressive language skills. By pausing between sentences, changing intonation, and correlating inflection with variances in punctuation within the text, the teacher effectively models the relationship between English grammatical patterns in written and spoken language.

24. C: Phonic awareness, or phonics (A), is knowing how alphabet letters correspond to speech sounds and vice versa. Awareness of phonetics (B) is knowing specific individual variations in speech sounds within a language. Phonemic (C) awareness is knowing the standard, general, or typical speech sounds used in a language. Alphabetic (D) awareness is knowing the written letter symbols representing speech sounds. (The alphabetic principle is the basis of phonics.)

25. D: According to research-based writing instruction strategies, when teachers assign students to small collaborative writing groups, they should set individual performance expectations for within-group as well as individual work. Teachers should also support student groups by providing them with structure. Classmates in collaborative writing groups should give each other both positive feedback for reinforcement and constructive feedback for correction as well.

26. B: In this paired reading strategy, which improves reading comprehension and helps students identify the main idea in informational text, after silently reading a text selection, the pair of students takes turns following these steps: One student paraphrases what he or she thinks the text's main idea is. The other student agrees or disagrees, explaining why. The pair then develops a consensus as to the text's main idea. Then they take turns finding details in the text that support its main idea.

27. B: Introducing sound-spellings (A) is for teaching students which written letters correspond to which spoken sounds, which they must know *before* learning to decode words. Discriminating individual phonemes within words (C) is for teaching students phonological awareness, which they also must have *before* decoding new words. Reviewing sound-spellings to overlearn them (D) is for phonics maintenance rather than word decoding. Blending phonemes into words (B) is for helping students learn a strategy to apply their sound-spelling learning to decoding unfamiliar words.

28. D: Research shows that phonics instruction is more effective than no phonics instruction, and also that it is more effective when it is systematic and explicit then when it is not (A). Research also shows that it is equally effective for children of all socioeconomic levels (B), that it is more effective when introduced in kindergarten or first grade (C), and that it is more effective when it helps students understand why they are learning letter-sound relationships and helps them apply this learning (D) to reading and writing.

29. C: Bias occurs when a test disadvantages a certain group of students. Including questions with cultural references that only a select group of students will understand disadvantages other students who do not understand the references. Students may miss these questions, despite having the reading skills the test is supposed to measure. Validity refers to whether the test measures what it is supposed to measure. Reliability relates to consistency of the test results over time and between participants.

30. B: Guided reading refers to a technique in which students work in a small group setting with the teacher, paraprofessional, or other educator to promote the development of reading comprehension and literacy skills. Students are typically grouped with others of the same or similar reading abilities and work closely with the educator to receive differentiated and individualized support when engaging with a text. While the specifics of implementing this strategy vary among groups and depend upon students' individual needs, guided reading groups typically follow a similar structure. Students begin by completing prereading activities to build background knowledge and provide context before reading the text independently. While reading, students respond to discussion questions prompted by the group facilitator and usually complete after-reading activities that are related to the text, building vocabulary, or specific concepts related to phonics instruction.

31. C: The ability to analyze the structure of words is necessary for vocabulary acquisition, decoding, and ultimately, reading comprehension. This skill becomes increasingly important as older students are exposed to more complex vocabulary, as it allows them to more effectively examine the parts of unfamiliar terms to derive meaning. Hands-on learning opportunities, such as word-building games, are beneficial in allowing students to physically manipulate the components of multisyllabic words, thus strengthening structural analysis skills.

32. A: Jason comments on the time in which the masterpieces were painted. Choice B is incorrect because the contents of the paintings are not described. Choice C is incorrect because he does not mention the artists. Choice D is incorrect because the architecture of the Uffizi Gallery is not mentioned.

33. A: According to the National Research Council (Snow, Burns, and Griffin, 1998), phonological awareness is the general ability to distinguish speech sounds from their meanings, whereas phonemic awareness is a more specific ability to distinguish individual speech sounds, i.e., phonemes, within words. Hence phonemic awareness is the most sophisticated level of phonological awareness (D). Therefore, choice B and C are also incorrect.

34. C: Researchers have found that instruction in simpler phonological skills like rhyming, onsets, and rimes may not have any direct benefits for reading development (A); however, they find that teaching these simpler skills first nevertheless can make it easier to teach the more complex ones *without* directly benefiting reading development (B). Researchers have also found that the phonological awareness instruction that appears most beneficial to subsequent reading development integrates blending and segmenting (C), not deleting and substituting (D).

35. C: Daniel has identified only external character traits, or traits related to the character's appearance. He has not identified any internal traits, or traits related to the character's thoughts, feelings, words, or actions. An appropriate next step would be to help Daniel differentiate between the two types of traits and find examples of each in the text. The remaining options would require Daniel to identify internal traits using textual evidence. For example, it would be difficult to describe how the character has changed throughout the story without using any internal traits to describe her at different points in the story. Similarly, it would be difficult to label the role she plays or compare her with other characters without using any internal traits to support the responses.

36. A: When planning instruction, the teacher must consider the general developmental level of students relative to their age group and recognize and accommodate individual differences in abilities and learning needs. Second-grade students can reasonably be expected to construct meaning from developmentally appropriate nonfiction texts, including multi-paragraph informational articles. In choosing such an article for a lesson focused on identifying main ideas, as well as supplementing new vocabulary with scaffolded definitions and examples, this teacher selects instructional materials that both align with state academic standards and meet students' developmental needs in language and literacy.

37. B: This exercise promotes students comprehension by requiring them to examine the authors' use of setting, plot, pacing, word choice, syntactical structures, narration, mood, metaphors, point of view, voice, and character development to find ways in which they are similar as well as different. In so doing, the students are discovering that language shapes meaning in ways both subtle and profound.

38. C: When students match picture cards with the consonant blends they begin with, they are using their understanding of the relationships between letters and the sounds they make. Therefore, it is a phonics activity. Choice A is a phonological awareness activity because it deals with sounds rather than letter/sound relationships. Choice B is a letter identification activity because students are matching letters to their names without addressing the sounds they make. Choice D is a comprehension activity because students are listening to a story and identifying story elements. They are not decoding the text independently.

39. C: Decoding, fluency, and comprehension are interrelated. The student is likely spending a lot of mental energy trying to decode unknown words, leaving little energy left to focus on comprehension. Additionally, repeatedly stopping to decode words interrupts fluency. This may cause the reader to struggle to make connections between the disjointed words and sentences. Implicit phonics instruction is not the best intervention option, as research has shown that systematic and explicit phonics instruction is most effective. Additionally, there is not enough information available to determine the cause of the student's decoding difficulties. Therefore, it cannot be assumed that it is related to a lack of phonological awareness skills or a language processing disorder.

40. B: Students reflect in reader response journals after independent, not sustained silent, reading (A). Teachers can use journals to monitor student reading, check comprehension, discuss texts, and suggest additional books (B). Not all students know how to respond to text by writing. Teachers should initially model the process, including prompts, and post lists of these, model methods for generating personal topics without prompts through the year, and give students lists of these for reference (C) to keep in their journals. Teachers should advise students to read about 80 percent of the time and write about 20 percent of the time (D).

41. A: Progress monitoring is a type of assessment used to track students' progress towards certain goals over time. When students are receiving reading interventions, frequent progress monitoring should be done to assess their progress and determine if the interventions are succeeding. Screening is done initially to determine if students are at risk for academic difficulties, and it is done at greater intervals, such as the start of each school year. Summative assessment occurs at the end of a unit of study or other larger unit of instruction. Norm referenced tests compare students' performances to the performances of sample groups of similar students, while progress monitoring is done to assess students' progress towards their own personal goals.

42. C: In choice C, the student selected a word that makes sense in the sentence but does not share any visual similarities with the existing word. He was relying on meaning to decode the word. Choice A demonstrates a structural error, as the student changed the verb ending. However, the sentence he read still sounds right. Choice B demonstrates a visual error, as he substituted a word that is visually similar to the existing word. Choice D demonstrates an insertion, as he added a prepositional phrase to the end of the sentence.

43. A: Tier-two vocabulary words are high-frequency and challenging words that hold a lot of meaning within the text. Because they appear frequently, not knowing their meanings can affect comprehension in multiple texts. High-frequency, concrete nouns are tier-one words. These are usually learned through everyday interactions and do not require explicit instruction. Domain-specific words are tier-three words. While it is beneficial for students to learn and use these words in some academic and professional contexts, they are unlikely to appear in everyday texts. Student-selected words may be used to generate interest in the topic and help students become actively involved in their learning. However, there is no guarantee that students will choose high-frequency words.

44. B: By assigning students a task that will require them to focus on key pieces of information in the text, the teacher is helping students set a purpose for reading. She is not asking the students why the author wrote the book, which would encourage them to consider the author's purpose. Choice C is incorrect because she did not ask students what they already know about the topic of water conservation. Choice D is incorrect because she did not ask students to compare or contrast this text with any other texts they have read.

45. A: Flexible grouping refers to the temporary and strategic grouping of students to address specific needs or develop particular skills in a given area. This strategy is beneficial in differentiating instruction to accommodate variances in abilities, learning styles, and developmental levels. Flexible groupings can be either homogenous, in which students are grouped with others of the same or similar abilities, or heterogenous, in which students of varying skill levels work together. In this situation, homogenous flexible groupings would help with scaffolding instruction to align with students' individual needs. This would allow the teacher to provide leveled texts according to students' levels of literacy skill development to effectively promote fluency and support reading comprehension.

46. C: A complex sentence has at least one dependent and one independent clause. A dependent clause cannot stand alone as a sentence, while an independent clause can. In choice C, the dependent clause is, "Before going to school"; while the independent clause is, "Michael brushed his teeth." Choice A is a simple sentence containing one independent clause. Choice B is a sentence with a compound predicate. Choice D is a compound sentence, meaning it contains two or more independent clauses joined by a coordinating conjunction or semicolon.

47. A: Recent research shows that dyslexia and similar reading disorders are primarily neurodevelopmental in origin, i.e., mainly due to neurological and developmental rather than environmental factors. Environmental deprivation of early exposure to reading activities can delay literacy development, but most (85 percent of) diagnosed learning problems are based in difficulties with reading and other language skills.

48. D: One way that a reader can determine that an informational text author may have had a hidden agenda is if the author's stated purposes for writing contradict other parts of the text. When the reader can identify motivations the author has not stated, the reader is better able to evaluate how effective the text is, whether they agree or disagree with it, and why. It is equally true that knowing author purpose enables readers to know what to expect from text, that knowing author motivation helps with reading for relevant details, and that knowing authors' purposes and motivations facilitates critical reader evaluation of author and text. However, a potential hidden agenda is most related to the importance of discovering unstated author purposes for evaluating text.

49. D: Decoding unfamiliar words when reading primarily involves understanding the structure, meaning, and the relationship between letters and sounds. Syntactic (e.g. syntax) refers to word order and sentence structure, which is necessary to interpret the meaning of phrases in context. Semantics refers to word meaning and has a very direct role in decoding meaning when encountering word roots. Graphophonic refers to written words and how the written form corresponds to the oral form of a word. To adequately read and recognize unfamiliar words, a reader needs to be able to sound out and possible recognize patterns that they have encountered elsewhere. With each of these systems activated, readers are able to succeed when encountering many unfamiliar words. However, the pragmatic domain, which deals with the use of language in social contexts and the rules for effective communication, does not directly contribute to the process of decoding written words.

50. C: While individual children develop oral language skills at different rates, early childhood students can reasonably be expected to communicate clearly and intelligibly when speaking. Difficulties with enunciation impede clear communication, and therefore, struggling students would benefit from individualized instruction focused on the foundations of phonics patterns. Such an intervention should include a variety of activities, such as having the student practice individual letter and word sounds with a focus on areas of difficulty, as well as reading aloud rhymes, familiar texts, and sentences that incorporate words the student has trouble enunciating. Students that continue to struggle may require a more intensive intervention, such as working with a speech and language pathologist.

51. A: An effective way to teach students the difference between denotation and connotation is to provide example sentences and have students choose a given word that best expresses the connotation of a highlighted word in each sentence. For example, to show the connotation of the word *challenge*, an example sentence "This is one of the many challenges that must be faced in order to solve the problem" could be given, and students could choose whether the connotation suggested by "challenges" in this case was "threats," "obstacles," "criticisms," or "setbacks." This instructional strategy is summarized in choice A, which is the correct answer. Since words generally have denotations and may or may not have connotations depending on their use, a Venn diagram would be misleading, and choice B is incorrect. Choice C is also incorrect, as highlighting words in a passage would not require students to distinguish between denotations and connotations, nor even to identify the exact connotations of words in context. Choice D would not be logical, since not all words have an emotional connotation, and the definition alone will be of little use for determining the connotations of a specific use of a word.

52. B: The keywords in choice B are used to signal how two or more items are the same and different, which is the purpose of compare-and-contrast texts. The keywords in choice A would likely be found in descriptive texts. The keywords in choice C would likely be found in cause-and-effect texts. The keywords in choice D would likely be found in sequential texts.

53. B: Including a word bank assists struggling readers with completing the activity by providing them with options to choose from. It is a way of scaffolding the activity while still requiring students to use context clues to determine which word is the best fit in each sentence. Providing the first few letters of each answer offers a bigger hint and may allow the student to guess the word easily. Cloze reading activities can be done in pairs, but it is possible that one student may supply the answer for the struggling reader. It is also possible for struggling readers to complete more than three questions with appropriate scaffolding.

54. D: During informal assessment for print concept awareness, a young child who cannot read yet should be able to identify where the teacher would start reading the book aloud (A), the title of the book (B), the meaning of a period as the end of a sentence in the book (C), a word in or on the book as well as a letter within a word in the book and spaces between words in the book, and the front, back, and directionality of the book.

55. D: In the children's information book genre, each book typically provides information devoted to a single topic of interest whereby children can learn facts about the topic and/or obtain answers to their many questions. Children's fiction (A) is a genre including mostly story books (B) featuring narratives with settings, plots, characters, and themes. Children's poetry books (C) feature a variety of topics presented in verse form.

56. C: The student has spelled all of the words correctly except for those with silent letters. Therefore, it would be most helpful to focus on silent-letter spelling patterns. Additionally, the student had no errors in subject/verb agreement.

57. C: Motivation, i.e., how interested students are in reading and in what ways (e.g., genres, subject matter, reading levels, etc.), is a psychological factor that influences not only whether or how much students read but also their comprehension. Attention (A) is a prerequisite for comprehension, problems with visual and auditory perception (C) can cause reading problems, and working memory (D) is required for word decoding and reading comprehension. Unlike motivation, these three are all cognitive factors.

58. A: "Conceptual vocabulary" terms are related in meaning and often have complex meanings. For instance, the term *community* may refer simply to a group of people living in close proximity to one another. However, there are many ideas that can be associated with this concept: neighbors, helping, spending time with one another, roles within a community, and so on. Word webs can be used to show a central term and its related concepts, demonstrating the relationship between words based on meaning. Using this type of graphic organizer provides a tangible way to show students that some words have complex meanings and are interconnected with other aspects of language.

59. C: Effective literacy instruction is differentiated to align with students' diverse learning needs. By varying instructional approaches, learning activities, and assessments, teachers can meet students where they are in terms of development and build upon their knowledge for continuous growth. Incorporating learning stations into the classroom is a highly effective method for providing student-centered learning experiences because they allow teachers to implement multiple activities simultaneously to accommodate varying learning styles, abilities, and interests. For literacy instruction specifically, this versatile approach can be used to strengthen students' skills in a particular area. In this situation, the teacher differentiates literacy instruction by creating four stations related to phonics instruction and further individualizes learning by assigning stations based upon areas in which each student needs improvement.

60. B: On a continuum, the simplest level of phonological awareness is represented by being able to recognize and produce rhymes in songs, and show understanding that sentences contain individual words by segmenting them (D). Segmenting words into syllables and blending syllables into words (A) represents a more complex level around the middle of the continuum. A higher level of complexity is segmenting words into onsets and rimes and blending onsets and rimes into words (C). The highest level is phonemic awareness, i.e., understanding that words contain individual phonemes and being able to manipulate (blend, segment, delete, substitute) these (B).

61. C: As the National Council of Teachers of English (NCTE) and International Literacy Association (ILA) point out, multiple researchers have found that the more experience students acquire with reading various literary genres, the more success they realize with writing in various genres (A). Experts find that analyzing various literary genres enables students to apply similar, not different (B), strategies and skills (e.g., identifying themes) across genres, promoting cognitive development (C). Genre studies expose students to many genres, which is more important than in-depth study of only one or two (D).

62. D: According to experts, teachers can model appropriate listening and speaking behaviors for students when they facilitate book discussions and during everyday conversations with them (A), when giving instruction to both whole classes and small groups (B), in one-to-one conversations they have with students and during classroom media discussions (C), and by thinking aloud specifically about the content they are teaching (D).

63. B: *Activating* is the term experts use to identify the reading strategy whereby the reader activates prior knowledge and applies it to the new information in reading to construct meaning from it. *Inferring* is a strategy whereby the reader combines what the text states explicitly with what it does not state but implies, and combines these both with what s/he already knows to draw inferences. *Questioning* is the reading strategy whereby the reader engages in "learning dialogues" with the text, author, classmates, and teachers to ask and answer questions about the text. *Summarizing* is the reading strategy whereby the reader paraphrases or restates what s/he perceives as the text's meaning.

64. A: According to researchers (cf. Cooper 1999, Diamond-CORE 2006), the challenges of changing teacher beliefs regarding reading instruction and initiating a new, research-based reading program arise during the first year of implementation (A). The challenges of refining that new approach, and ensuring that teachers and other staff adhere to program design and implement it consistently, arise in the second year (C). The challenge of addressing teacher "domestication" of a new reading program arises during the third year (A). These experts do not address implementation's fourth year (D); the first three are more challenging.

65. B: There are many, many factors that affect reading comprehension in various proportions, depending on the student. Generally speaking, students must be able to recognize vocabulary, decode unfamiliar words, and monitor their own understanding in order to comprehend a given text. In Choice A, all of these factors could affect comprehension; written language development and breakfast, however, are probably less important than the set of factors in Choice B. In Choice C, the factors seem to relate primarily to a student's understanding of the words in the text—vocabulary, sight words, and the ability to look up words. However, students must understand more than simply the words on the page; they must understand the relationships between the words and the underlying meaning of the whole text. In Choice D, classroom participation and performance in other subjects does not necessarily indicate or affect comprehension skills.

66. A: A story map outlines the main elements of the story, including the characters, setting, conflict, plot, and resolution. Recording these elements will assist the student in remembering and analyzing the story after it has been read. If the student has retention issues, he or she may not recall the story elements even after reading the story twice or listening to an audio version. A KWL chart can be used to activate prior knowledge and help the student reflect on what was learned, but it does not outline the story elements needed to analyze plot.

67. C: She should locate the vowels, then locate familiar word parts. Syllables are organized around vowels. In order to determine the syllables, this student should begin by locating the vowels. It's possible to have a syllable that is a single vowel (*a/gain)*. It isn't possible to have a syllable that is a single consonant. Once the word has been broken into its component syllables the reader is able to study the syllables to find ones that are familiar and might give her a clue as to the word's meaning, such as certain prefixes or suffixes.

68. A: In shared writing experiences, students share thoughts during a class discussion, and the teacher records them on paper. Because students are in the preliterate stage of writing, they are not yet using sound/symbol relationships to spell words. Writing at this stage may resemble scribbling or contain strings of pretend letters. If Mr. Suarez records the students' thoughts for this activity, the story can be reread multiple times. If students write independently or with partners, it will be difficult to maintain the message of the story each time it is reread. Similar difficulties would occur with interactive writing because students help write the shared story on paper.

69. C: The words in this set can be grouped into two categories: academic vocabulary and content vocabulary. Academic vocabulary words are commonly used in school but are not specific to one subject area. For example, students may compare shapes in math, compare living things in science, and compare characters in reading. Content vocabulary refers to words related to one specific subject area. *Organism*, *cell*, and *habitat* are typically used in science.

70. A: Story maps are a form of graphic organizer that provides students with a visual aid to more effectively record and recall important details from a text. This resource is versatile, and can be differentiated to align with students' grade level, as well as variances in literacy skills. Story maps can be completed independently, and help students identify key components of a text, thus promoting reading comprehension and the ability to retell stories by recalling major details.

71. A: While all of these options are important and beneficial for reading development, research has indicated that phonemic awareness is one of the strongest predictors of early reading success. Understanding that words are made up of individual sounds assists with learning the letter/sound relationships in phonics. These relationships are used to decode words.

72. C: Embarrassing students in front of classmates and/or punishing them do NOT prevent, but actually incite, individual and group student rebellion. Showing interest in student work and encouraging students (A), alerting students to change their behaviors through physical proximity and touch (B), and reminding students of times when they succeeded and modifying lesson presentations (D) to be more interesting than any distractors are all low-impact teacher interventions that prevent undesirable student behaviors from escalating.

73. D: Implicit phonics instruction uses a whole-to-part approach, with students reading whole texts rather than starting with isolated phonemes. Students learn to recognize whole words by sight. Through analyzing and comparing words, they then discover phonics and spelling patterns. A benefit is that students read authentic texts and learn in a meaningful context rather than practicing skills in isolation. However, research has shown that explicit phonics instruction, which progresses from part to whole, leads to stronger decoding, spelling, and comprehension skills.

74. C: In the transitional stage of writing development, children begin to use capital and lowercase letters appropriately. They know how to spell many high-frequency words correctly and use knowledge of sound-symbol relationships to record the sounds they hear in more complex words. In choice C, the student has spelled the word almost correctly, using the *e* to represent the /ē/ formed by a *y* in the actual spelling of the word. Choice A demonstrates the preliterate stage of writing, where children use scribbles that are intended as writing. Choice B represents the emergent stage of writing, when children begin to form letters correctly. In this stage, they often write in all capital letters. At first, random strings of letters are used. Later, some sounds, such as the first and last sounds, may be represented correctly. Choice D demonstrates the fluent stage of writing development, where most words are spelled conventionally.

75. D: To establish literacy-rich environments, experts advise teachers to label everything in the classroom with words and pictures. This helps students connect all things and places with written language representing them, rather than distracts (A). Directions, calendars, signs, and schedules are not only everyday organizational tools; teachers can also have students use them to understand everyday language use (B). Word and picture labels should not be avoided, but should include textured materials, Braille, large fonts, etc., enabling access for visually impaired students (C). If teachers and students redesign classrooms to reflect themes or books they have studied, students "live in" lessons, experiencing them directly (D).

76. D: Research-based vocabulary instruction findings show that children need ample word repetition, but not through drilling. Multiple exposures to the same words in different contexts are more effective. Multiple and repeated exposures are important because children do not learn vocabulary through only one or two exposures to a new word. Research finds that they do not simply learn vocabulary in texts indirectly from reading; instead, teachers must give them direct instruction in the new vocabulary words they find in their texts.

77. D: Prosody refers to reading with appropriate intonation, rhythm, and stress. Because Liz is reading in a monotone voice and not using appropriate phrasing, it would be beneficial for her teacher to focus on prosody during small-group instruction. Her accuracy rate is in the independent range, which demonstrates she has strong word recognition skills. Her high accuracy rate also suggests she is already reading with automaticity.

78. A: Phonemic substitution is a phonological awareness skill that refers to the ability to recognize the creation of a new word when one sound is replaced with another. Understanding this concept is necessary for the development of reading comprehension and spelling skills, so it must be taught explicitly. By using color-coded letter cards to spell vocabulary words and replace individual sounds, the teacher shows students how phonemic substitution is used to create new words. This strategy also supports students' recognition of the relationship between phonemic awareness and phonics, as it allows them to visualize the substitution of individual letters to produce new sounds and words.

79. A: The student is adjusting his language according to his current social situation. When speaking to a friend, he uses informal language. When presenting a report in front of the class and teacher, he switches to more formal language. Cultural context refers to the ways that messages are delivered and received based on differing cultural backgrounds and norms. Contextual clues are clues in a text that assist readers with determining the meanings of unknown words. Personal context refers to how communication is affected by an individual's age, gender, educational background, and other personal factors.

80. A: Choice A is correct because the author of an informational text may have ulterior motives for writing a text but not state these explicitly. Choice B is incorrect because some authors may not explicitly state every purpose of writing a text. Choice C is incorrect because the main idea of a text is what the reader should understand from it, whereas the purpose of a text is why the author writes the text. Choice D is incorrect because identifying unstated author purposes affords a number of advantages to readers, including the ability to judge the effectiveness of the text, whether or not they agree with the text, and why they agree or disagree with the text.

81. D: Analogies are used to help students recognize the relationships between words. Students are commonly given a pair of words whose relationship they must first identify. They then apply the same type of relationship to complete another word pair. Analogies can be used to help students recognize many different types of relationships, including recognizing synonyms, antonyms, and more. While students may explore word structure, definitions, and origins while completing analogies, the overall objective of analogies is to recognize and apply relationships between sets of words.

82. A: From a literature review, researchers (c. Henderson and Mapp, 2002) concluded that students whose families are involved in their learning get higher grades, take more advanced classes, have higher graduation rates, and are more likely to attend postsecondary education. Students perform best academically when their parents adopt varied roles in their learning, like not only participating in school events and activities, but also helping at home, contributing to key school program decisions, guiding children through the system, etc. (B). Students with involved families also attend school more regularly, have more positive attitudes toward school, and demonstrate better behavior in school (C). Finally, students from diverse backgrounds perform better academically from school-family collaboration to bridge cultural gaps (D).

83. B: Decoding is the ability to recognize and pronounce written language by correctly sounding out the letters within words. Selecting age-appropriate learning materials is important in designing instruction that builds this emergent literacy skill to ultimately promote reading comprehension and fluency. Young children learn best through active, hands-on learning experiences, implementing kinesthetic activities in literacy instruction helps to strengthen connections and increase retention. In this situation, having students cut and paste letters to create multisyllabic words allows them to physically interact with learning materials, promoting their understanding of letter-sound relationships to build decoding skills.

84. C: When a word can be pronounced two different ways, reading the sentence twice and pronouncing the word each way can help the reader determine which pronunciation makes sense. For example, a student might encounter a sentence that says, "The mother put a bow in her daughter's hair." Knowing that *bow* can be pronounced two different ways, the student can read the sentence twice, pronouncing the word differently each time. That strategy should help the student identify which way makes sense. Choices A and B are incorrect because identifying known parts of the word using visual clues will not assist the reader with knowing which pronunciation is correct in the given context. Additional context clues from the surrounding text are needed. Choice D is incorrect because the student may know other *oo* words with both pronunciations, so again, additional context clues are needed.

85. C: When a student has trouble recognizing words out of context (A), this is mainly a sign that the student has problems with decoding words, as is slow, laborious oral reading (B). Having trouble differentiating main ideas or important information from minor details (C) in text is mainly a sign that the student has problems with reading comprehension. Having trouble relating text to his or her own existing knowledge (D) often reflects difficulty using background knowledge, which can influence comprehension but is conceptually distinct from basic comprehension skills such as identifying main ideas.

86. A: One good indication of print awareness in a young child during informal assessment is that the child can identify the front and back of a book. Another is that the child can identify one letter in a word in the book, not all letters in words (B). Another is that the child can identify both words in a book, and the spaces between them (C). Print awareness in a young child does not mean the child can read sentences fluently (D), or even words yet: awareness of print concepts is a prerequisite for learning to read.

87. D: While all children will acquire literacy skills at individual rates, there are general developmental characteristics associated with each age group. Recognizing atypical patterns of development is essential to identifying potential delays or learning disabilities so as to provide early intervention. By third grade, most neurotypical students have developed the ability to recognize and spell high-frequency sight words and write with a degree of accuracy and fluency. In this situation, the student is displaying possible signs of dyslexia, which is a learning disability that can significantly impede literacy skill development, particularly in the domains of reading and writing, if not properly addressed. As such, upon noticing these signs, it is important that the teacher refer this student for an initial evaluation to determine the need for special education services. Doing so will help to ensure he receives the supports and accommodations necessary to promote his literacy skill development.

88. C: Understanding basic concepts of print is a fundamental skill for emergent literacy development in young children. While most prekindergarten students have not yet learned to read fluently, it is still important to demonstrate the prevalence and application of printed language in daily life. This includes teaching young children about the purpose and use of printed books. Modeling how to hold a book, turn pages, read from left to right, and pointing out key characteristics, such as a book's title, cover, and author's name, develops print awareness in prekindergarten students. Doing so promotes students' understanding that books contain printed words that convey meaning, establishing a foundation for emergent literacy development.

89. C: Educational researchers (cf. Pardede, 2011) observe that novels can be too long for public school classes to read in limited time (A). Students typically require extensive instruction and time to understand figurative devices and other unfamiliar language in poems (B). Though students can be assigned to read drama, it is often impracticable for crowded classes with limited hours to act out a play (D). In contrast, short stories (C) can be read in one sitting and typically have one plot, fewer characters than novels, and brief, not detailed, setting descriptions, making it easier for students to follow a storyline.

90. B: Anticipation guides are tools that are used to activate prior knowledge and help students build interest in a topic before reading. They typically consist of a series of statements about the topic, and students choose whether they agree or disagree with each statement. During reading, students note if newly learned information is changing their initial responses, and they reevaluate their initial responses after reading. A storyboard is a graphic organizer that shows individual scenes from a story in order. Concept maps are visual representations of the relationships between concepts, often displayed using a web-like format. An outline is a list of the main topics, subtopics, and details contained in the text.

Practice Test #2

1. National research data show which of these about the relationship of high school reading and academic achievement to parental involvement?

a. Students resent parents' checking their homework as an invasion of privacy.
b. Students often get higher English grades when parents discuss school plans.
c. Students rebel in adolescence against high parent educational expectations.
d. Students find discussing future plans with parents to cause undue pressure.

2. A teacher wants to work on her students' listening comprehension in addition to their reading comprehension since she understands that the skills are interrelated. She has a series of short stories that she thinks the students will enjoy. Which of the following would be the best supplement to typical written comprehension exercises?

a. Preview the content and then read the stories aloud to the students. Assess listening comprehension through verbal and written questions.
b. Ask the students to choose one story each to read aloud to a small group. Encourage the students to discuss what they have learned afterward.
c. Assign each student a story to read and require them to write a report on it. Each student should then present his or her report based on what he or she has learned to the class.
d. Have the students read stories aloud to the class, and create mock tests based upon the main ideas which they identify.

3. A first-grade teacher has noticed that one student struggles to recall stories in the correct sequence. The student often mixes up events from the beginning, middle, and end of the story, and confuses important connecting details. Which of the following strategies would likely best support this student's language skill development in this area?

a. Fostering personal connections between the student's life and events from stories
b. Providing the student aids such as graphic organizers, story maps, and pictures that correspond with events from stories
c. Exposing the student to a variety of texts relevant to her personal interests
d. Reading aloud to the student individually and asking open-ended questions about the story

4. Which statement best describes phonemic awareness?

a. Phonemic awareness is the ability to identify and manipulate sounds at the sentence level.
b. Phonemic awareness is the ability to identify and manipulate sounds at the word level.
c. Phonemic awareness is the ability to identify and manipulate sounds at the syllable level.
d. Phonemic awareness is the ability to identify and manipulate sounds at the phoneme level.

5. A teacher is introducing a new phonics skill to her students. She begins with explicit instruction on the skill, followed by modeling. Which instructional component should come next?

a. Independent practice
b. Guided practice
c. Generalization
d. Feedback

6. During a phonics assessment, a second-grade teacher has students individually read aloud from a list that includes both high-frequency and nonsense multisyllabic words. By including nonsense words on the list, the teacher is most likely evaluating which of the following skills?

a. Decoding and blending
b. Identifying rhyming and alliteration
c. Segmenting and substituting phonemes
d. Counting syllables

7. For an instructional activity to develop phonological awareness in K-1 students, which of these would teach them segmentation on multiple phonological levels?

a. Teaching children how to separate sentences into the individual words that make up each sentence
b. Teaching children to divide sentences into words, words into syllables, and syllables into phonemes
c. Teaching children to divide words into individual syllables, or to divide words into onsets and rimes
d. Teaching children how to separate short, monosyllabic words into individual component phonemes

8. When should students learn how to decode?

a. Decoding is the most basic and essential strategy to becoming a successful reader. It should be introduced to kindergartners during the first two weeks of school.
b. Decoding is not a teachable skill. It is an unconscious act and is natural to all learners.
c. Decoding should be taught only after children have mastered every letter–sound relationship as well as every consonant digraph and consonant blend. They should also be able to recognize and say the 40 phonemes common to English words and be able to recognize at least a dozen of the most common sight words.
d. Decoding depends on an understanding of letter–sound relationships. As soon as a child understands enough letters and their correspondent sounds to read a few words, decoding should be introduced.

9. Among instructional strategies that aid in student comprehension of nonfictional text, which of these is most useful for promoting critical thinking?

a. Answering open-ended questions about texts
b. Skimming the text for features that give signs
c. Establishing connections between text and life
d. Establishing connections between text and self

10. A teacher gives students an unfamiliar text. Without doing a picture walk or pre-teaching any vocabulary words, she asks them to read it once independently. During this first reading, students are told to identify the overall meaning of the text, as well as note their initial impressions. Students discuss these responses with their peers. The teacher then asks the students to read a specific portion of the text a second time, analyzing the author's use of figurative language. Students then discuss their thoughts again. The teacher then asks the students to reread the text a third time, comparing and contrasting the main character with the main character in another text they have read. Students once again share their responses with peers. Which type of reading activity does this example demonstrate?

a. Guided reading
b. SQ3R
c. Close reading
d. Scanning

11. Of the following, which represents an indirect way in which students receive instruction in and learn vocabulary?

a. Being exposed repeatedly to vocabulary in multiple teaching contexts
b. Being exposed to vocabulary when adults read aloud to them
c. Being pre-taught specific words found in text prior to reading
d. Being taught vocabulary words over extended periods of time

12. Abi, a fifth-grader, is reading aloud to his teacher during one-on-one reading time. His teacher uses this time to evaluate ongoing fluency and comprehension skills. Following today's reading, Abi's teacher determines that he needs practice with words that begin with digraphs. Which of the following sets of words would most likely be part of this assignment?

a. Chicken, Shells, That
b. Were, Frame, Click
c. Sponge, Think, Blank
d. Packed, Blistered, Smoothed

13. Elizabeth, a sixth-grade student, is researching Hellen Keller's life before writing a biographical report about her. The report will include information about both her childhood and adulthood, along with information about how she learned to communicate over time. When selecting books to use as sources and while writing her own report, which type of text structure would best fit her purposes?

a. Cause and effect
b. Time-order
c. Compare and contrast
d. Descriptive

14. A teacher has challenged a student with a book about Antarctica that is just beyond the high end of the student's Instructional level. The teacher points out that the student already knows quite a bit about penguins because the class studied them earlier in the year. He reminds the student that she's recently seen a television show about the seals that also live in Antarctic waters. The teacher gives the student a list of words she's likely to find in the text, and they discuss what those words might mean. The student begins to read, but stops to ask the teacher what *circumpolar* means. The teacher is also unfamiliar with the word, but reminds her that *circum* is a prefix. The student recalls that it means "about or around" and deduces that circumpolar most likely refers to something found around or in a polar region. This instructional approach is called:

a. Modular instruction
b. Scaffolding
c. Linking
d. Transmutation

15. A teacher wants to introduce the concept of connotative and denotative meanings while reading a novel. He plans to use character traits as a way to introduce this topic. Which set of words to describe a character would best help him introduce and explain connotative and denotative word meanings?

a. Kind and nice
b. Happy and joyful
c. Determined and persistent
d. Frugal and cheap

16. As a reading strategy, ELA teachers can best give students practice in making predictions to support comprehension through which activity?

a. Predicting what or whom a book is about
b. Predicting what a novel's character will do
c. Predicting a significant event in a narrative
d. Predicting (B) and/or (C), rather than (A)

17. Which of the following is the most effective way for a first-grade teacher to enhance students' reading proficiency?

a. Provide effective phonics instruction
b. Encourage oral storytelling in the classroom
c. Replace basal texts with real literature
d. Have students make daily visits to the school library

18. Which statement accurately reflects a principle regarding self-questioning techniques for increasing student reading comprehension?

a. Asking only what kinds of "expert questions" fit the text's subject matter
b. Asking only those questions that the text raises for the individual student
c. Asking how each text portion relates to chapter main ideas is unnecessary
d. Asking how the text information fits with what the student already knows

19. Which of the following instructional strategies likely best promotes development of phonemic awareness in early childhood students?

a. Providing multiple opportunities for students to engage in writing activities
b. Asking students to sequence the events of a story using pictures
c. Incorporating activities such as rhymes, songs, and alphabet games
d. Creating a print-rich environment using labels, word walls, posters, and bulletin boards

20. Some teachers suggest a simple visual graphic to teach younger and beginning reading students about the main idea and supporting details in nonfiction text: outline your hand on the board and have students follow suit (or give them prepared handouts with a hand outline). Label parts of the hand. Where on the hand drawing would the supporting details logically be?

a. On the thumb of the hand
b. On the fingers of the hand
c. On the palm of the hand
d. On the back of the hand

21. A review of the research literature has found which of the following about the influence of continuing family involvement in education on students in grades 6-12?

a. Middle school and high school students with involved families adjust to new schools like others.
b. Middle school and high school students with involved families always increase the work quality.
c. Middle school and high school students with involved families make more realistic future plans.
d. Middle school and high school students with involved families have equal odds of dropping out.

22. Children first begin their vocabulary development using which skill?

a. Reading
b. Writing
c. Listening
d. Speaking

23. A second-grade teacher wants to measure students' progress toward reaching academic benchmarks related to expressing opinions through writing. Which of the following assessment practices would be most effective in informally evaluating this skill?

a. Reviewing students' responses to journal prompts focused on opinion writing
b. Measuring students' accuracy as they complete sentence dictation exercises
c. Observing students as they peer-edit one another's writing
d. Administering a brief constructed-response exam on a variety of writing topics

24. Which statement is most accurate about reader identification of author purpose in informational writing?

a. Considering why an author wrote a text affords greater insights to it.
b. Considering why an author wrote a text weakens critical reading skills.
c. Considering why an author wrote a text frees the reader from expectations.
d. Considering why an author wrote a text causes a weaker connection with the text.

25. A student is reading a fictional book and has difficulty decoding the word *maple*. Which spelling pattern could the teacher explain to help the student decode this word and similar words in the future?

a. Vowel digraph pairs
b. R-controlled vowels
c. Closed syllables
d. Open syllables

26. A third-grade teacher is planning a lesson in which students will independently read an informational text. Prior to beginning the lesson, the teacher will review new vocabulary words and add them to the class word wall. As students read the text, they will fill out a guided summary frame. Afterward, students will discuss their summaries with a table partner. These strategies are likely intended to promote students' skills in which of the following areas?

a. Irregular sight word recognition
b. Using text features to locate information
c. Comprehension of academic language
d. Understanding the relationship between written and spoken language

27. A fourth-grade teacher has just completed a unit focused on writing narratives, and wants to determine whether students mastered the concept of using transitional phrases to organize events in a story. Which of the following assessment approaches would be most appropriate?

a. Administering a self-selected response exam
b. Assigning an oral presentation about an informational topic
c. Instructing students to write an original story
d. Assigning a research project on a topic of students' choosing

28. A student is reading a fictional book and reaches the following sentence: "Unlike Mark, whose college plans were tentative, Ana already had firm plans to attend the state university." Which type of context clue is present in this sentence to help the student determine the meaning of *tentative*?

a. Synonym clue
b. Definition clue
c. Antonym clue
d. Inference clue

29. What has research found about appropriately challenging, effective instruction for high achievers?

a. Low-income high achievers are less likely to attend college.
b. High achievers should be given highly directive assignments.
c. Students may collaborate across classes or even grade levels.
d. Differentiation requires more supports for the higher grades.

30. Aidan, a fifth-grade student, writes a letter to the cafeteria manager at his school asking her to implement a schoolwide composting program. He outlines reasons why the composting program would benefit the environment and save the school money on waste disposal costs. He ends his letter by politely asking her to consider the proposal. What is Aidan's primary purpose for writing?

a. To inform
b. To persuade
c. To entertain
d. To describe

31. As an assessment, a teacher gives a student a cloze procedure. Which response is an example of a student reading strategy based primarily on using syntactic cues to meaning?

a. The missing word must be "telescope" because it ends with the root "scope" and the context has to do with things that are far away.
b. The missing word must be a bad thing, because the word describing it is "horrible."
c. The missing word must be an adjective because it is before the word that is a noun.
d. The missing word must be impossible to guess, because I read one word at a time.

32. Teachers must consider student developmental levels when assigning cooperative learning projects and/or discussions. For example, students are bored by topics at younger age levels and lost by topics at older ones. In addition to chronological age, which other developmental level does this example relate to most?

a. Social developmental levels
b. Cognitive developmental levels
c. Emotional developmental levels
d. Behavioral developmental levels

33. A kindergarten teacher says the words *tap* and *top* aloud. She asks students to identify whether the sound that is different is found in the beginning, middle, or ending of the words. Which skill does this activity practice?

a. Phoneme substitution
b. Phoneme discrimination
c. Phoneme deletion
d. Phoneme insertion

34. When assessing error patterns in a student's reading, which is most detrimental to reading proficiency?

a. Substitution of "control" for "contrariness"
b. Substitution of "resistant" for "recalcitrant"
c. Substituting a noun, not a verb, for a noun
d. Substituting for errors informed by context

35. To help students find and use evidence from nonfictional text to support their ideas, which instructional strategy is most applicable?

a. Inquiry Charts (I-Charts)
b. Graphic organizers
c. Journaling
d. RAFT

36. Which of the following strategies would likely be most effective in developing awareness of the alphabetic principle among prekindergarten students?

a. Teaching the concepts of consonants and vowels separately
b. Introducing and focusing lessons on new letters and sounds individually, or a few at a time
c. Using rhyming games and songs to emphasize individual sounds within words
d. Using manipulatives to teach segmenting and blending of multisyllabic words

37. A prekindergarten teacher uses daily circle time for reading aloud to students. When introducing new vocabulary words from a text, the teacher pauses to explain their meaning, and adds them to the class word wall with corresponding pictures. After each read-aloud, the teacher also asks students to discuss their favorite parts of the story. By implementing these strategies, the teacher demonstrates understanding of which of the following?

a. Individual differences in developmental levels among young children
b. The role of receptive and expressive language in literacy development
c. Interventions for supporting literacy development in struggling students
d. The importance of differentiating instruction to align with individual students' needs

38. In the response to intervention (RTI) framework, which recommendations from the federal What Works Clearinghouse (WWC) apply to all three RTI tiers regarding primary-grades classroom reading instruction?

a. Intensive instruction
b. Small-group instruction
c. Differentiated instruction
d. Evidence-based instruction

39. Students in Ms. Dean's class discuss their existing knowledge and thoughts about sustainable farming practices before conducting any research on the topic. Next, they research the topic, locating four reputable print sources and conducting one interview with an expert in the field. They take notes, recording key information from each source. They use their notes from all of the sources to write a research report on the topic. They also complete a written reflection outlining how their initial thoughts have changed as a result of the new information gathered from the sources. Which comprehension strategy are students demonstrating?

a. Evaluating
b. Inferring
c. Drawing conclusions
d. Synthesizing

40. A fourth-grade teacher had her students write haiku in order to promote the students' __________.

a. reading comprehension
b. vocabulary
c. word identification skills
d. confidence

41. Regarding instruction in letter-sound associations for students having difficulty with naming or recall, which is a recommended instructional strategy?

a. They should progress to new material quickly to maintain learning momentum.
b. These students will forget associations without extensive practice.
c. Students will become bored and lose motivation with overlearning.
d. Every lesson should focus on new material instead of on reviewing.

42. To inform instructional strategies for writing mechanics, which of the following is an appropriate benchmark for students in grades 3-5?

a. Using periods after declarative sentences
b. Using question marks after interrogatives
c. Using commas to divide a series of words
d. Using quotation marks around quotations

43. Michael is a sixth-grade student who struggles to summarize fictional texts he has read. His summaries are often lengthy and include many unimportant details. Which type of graphic organizer could best help Michael develop concise summaries?

a. KWL charts
b. Semantic maps
c. Venn diagrams
d. Story maps

Refer to the following for question 44:

> Roger, a student with autism, is nonverbal but is in an inclusion classroom with a paraprofessional for support. The teacher, Ms. Schneider, has noticed that the paraprofessional has arrived late and appeared distracted over the past week. For tomorrow's upcoming lesson, Ms. Schneider is planning a group activity with the students.

44. After resolving the problem with the paraprofessional, what is an intervention that Ms. Schneider and the paraprofessional could put in place to support Roger with the upcoming group activity?

a. Pair him with another nonverbal student for group assignments
b. Tell the student to listen to other students in his group but tell him he does not have to participate
c. Excuse the student from all group activities
d. Provide a device to the student to assist him with communication

45. Researchers have found effective programs that promote independent reading share which common element(s)?

a. Active parental involvement is the one important element shared among all effective programs.
b. They focus on collaboration of other significant adults in students' lives rather than active parental involvement.
c. They all have access to varied material, community partnerships, parental involvement, and adult collaboration.
d. Partnerships among community institutions and access to varied material are the most important.

46. A fourth-grade teacher asks her students an open-ended question about the author's purpose relating to a novel they are reading. She gives students a few minutes to think about their personal responses before discussing them with partners for a few additional minutes. Finally, she asks students to discuss their responses as a class. Which instructional strategy is the teacher using?

a. Think-pair-share
b. Jigsaw
c. Close reading
d. Cloze reading

47. Which activity would be most appropriate to teach decoding of CVCe words?

a. Covering parts of the word
b. Chunking
c. Building word families
d. Blending

48. Which of the following teacher actions would most effectively encourage reading development in students' home environments?

a. Reminding students to read with their parents each day
b. Sending home a weekly update listing the phonics skills the class practiced
c. Sending home a list of weekly spelling words for students to memorize
d. Sending home leveled texts for students to read with family members

49. A teacher takes a running record while Charlie, a second grader, reads a new text. Part of the running record is shown below.

home (written above "house") / grumpy (written above "grouchy") / omission (written above "any")
The witch's house was deep in the woods, hidden behind some trees. A grouchy cat guarded the entrance to the house, hissing loudly when any strangers approached. Nobody had dared to go near it in years.

Which strategy would be most appropriate for the teacher to focus on during the next guided reading session?

a. Using semantic cues
b. Using syntactic cues
c. Monitoring omissions
d. Making self-corrections

50. A student incorrectly pronounces the word *rattle* with a long vowel *a*. The teacher explains a general rule to the student about splitting doubled consonants. This instructional strategy focuses most on using which of these?

a. Structural analysis
b. Spelling patterns
c. Syllabication
d. Morphemes

51. A third-grade teacher strives to incorporate opportunities for students to engage in reading, writing, speaking, and listening throughout the school day. For example, students keep an observation journal for science lessons, read grade-level-appropriate current-event articles in social studies, and frequently solve word problems during math lessons. Which of the following best describes how implementing these strategies is beneficial in creating a literate environment for students?

a. Promoting the development of expressive and receptive language skills
b. Differentiating instructional activities to meet students' learning preferences
c. Making overt connections between the curriculum and students' lives
d. Infusing literacy throughout the curriculum

52. Which of the following is an example of a summative assessment?

a. Final project critiques
b. Oral question-and-answer sessions
c. Running records
d. Pop quizzes

53. A teacher is working with a group of third graders at the same reading level. Her goal is to improve reading fluency. She asks each child in turn to read a page from a book about mammal young. She asks the children to read with expression. She also reminds them they don't need to stop between each word; they should read as quickly as they comfortably can. She cautions them, however, not to read so quickly that they leave out or misread a word. The teacher knows the components of reading fluency are:

a. Speed, drama, and comprehension
b. Cohesion, rate, and prosody
c. Understanding, rate, and prosody
d. Rate, accuracy, and prosody

54. In scientific informational texts, which of these are authors LEAST likely to do?

a. Explicitly state their point of view about the research they did
b. Explicitly state the purpose of the research they are reporting
c. Explicitly state their interpretation of the study evidence or data
d. Explicitly state which variables they investigated and in whom

55. Some of the students in Mr. Smith's fourth-grade class cannot decode words well enough to read fluently in class. He knows they are well behind grade level and that he needs to provide them with activities that will allow them to be successful, building skills and confidence at the same time. Which activity would be best for this purpose?

a. Enlist the parents' help by sending home a weekly list of sight words that the students can practice and memorize, decreasing the need to decode when they read.
b. Show the students how to create words out of movable alphabet tiles or magnetic letters, building (encoding) words as they sound them out.
c. Provide the children with early childhood readers that contain only very simple words so that the children will not feel badly as they read.
d. Allow those children having trouble to stop each time they reach a challenging word and sound it out carefully, recording it to a list that will be studied for homework.

56. What is the *most* accurate statement about dictionaries relative to denotative and connotative word meanings?

a. Dictionaries only provide denotative meanings of words.
b. Dictionaries may offer examples of both types of meaning.
c. Dictionaries only offer connotative meanings for words.
d. Dictionary definitions differ from denotative meanings.

57. For their monthly project, a group of students can choose to read and respond to one book on a list supplied by their teacher. The books are grouped according to genre. Most students choose books listed under the genre that is described as "modern-day stories that are not true, but seem as though they could really happen." Which genre did most of the students choose from?

a. Historical fiction
b. Autobiography
c. Realistic fiction
d. Fantasy

58. A teacher wants to select books for her emergent readers to add to the classroom library. Which set of text features are most appropriate for emergent readers?

a. Predictable text placement, repetition, and picture support
b. Complex and varied sentence types, multiple sentences per page, little picture support
c. Sidebars and charts, several lines of text per page, descriptive words and phrases
d. Complex text structures, figurative language, technical vocabulary words

59. After students have read the first chapter of a book, their teacher asks them to speculate on what the main character is going to do next. The students are being asked to use a comprehension strategy called:

a. Summarizing
b. Monitoring and correcting
c. Making predictions
d. Drawing conclusions

60. Which of these accurately reflects a guideline for teaching phonemic awareness based on the research literature?

a. Explicit instruction in phonemic awareness is found to be required for all students.
b. Instruction should be driven by analysis of data from phonemic awareness testing.
c. Instruction in phonemic awareness is more effective when phonemes are implicit.
d. Effective phonemic awareness instruction is scaffolded identically for all students.

61. A sixth-grade science teacher wants to help his students recognize connections between words containing the same Latin root. Which activity would most likely achieve this goal?

a. Defining words containing the root using a dictionary
b. Creating a semantic map
c. Searching for words containing the root in the science textbook
d. Comparing and contrasting words containing the root using a Venn diagram

62. A seventh grader has never had much success with reading. Her ability to decode is rudimentary; she stops and starts when reading, frequently loses her place, or misreads an important word. She doesn't seem aware of where errors occur, or she does not attempt to correct them. When asked about what she's read, her comprehension is minimal. To help her, instructional focus on which of the following would be most useful?

a. Carefully organized lessons in decoding, sight words, vocabulary, and comprehension at least three to five times a week. These mini-lessons must be extremely clear, with the parts broken down to the lowest common denominator. The more tightly interwoven and systematized the instruction, the better chance this student will have.
b. A weekly lesson focusing on one aspect of reading. This student will be overwhelmed if too many strategies are offered at once. The instruction should focus first on recognizing sight words, then letter–sound association. Next, the girl needs an understanding of the rules of syntax.
c. The student isn't trying. Her instruction should be aimed at helping her learn to be self-motivated and disciplined in her approach to learning.
d. Comprehension strategies will help her grasp the overall meaning of a text. From there she can begin to drill down until she's able to combine various approaches that, working together, will enable her to read.

63. Explicit instruction in reading comprehension strategies is found more effective in research. Which component of explicit instruction is reflected when a teacher reads text the students are reading while conducting a "think-aloud?"

a. Modeling
b. Application
c. Guided practice
d. Direct explanation

64. If a writer's purpose is to create portraits of people for a reading audience whose interest is in different personalities, motivations, and their expression in various behaviors and relationships, which mode of writing is most appropriate?

a. A fictional novel
b. A how-to manual
c. A persuasive essay
d. An explanatory paper

65. A parent of a first-grade student is concerned about her child's use of phonetic spelling. She is concerned that her daughter is not spelling enough words conventionally and is developing habits that will be difficult to overcome. She presents the following sentence that her daughter recently wrote as an example:

A leprd haz spots.

What would be the most appropriate response to the parent?

a. Going forward, an adult should assist the child during writing tasks and confirm the spelling of each unknown word.
b. Students in this stage typically write the sounds that they hear, and this stage is a stepping stone to conventional spelling development.
c. At this age, the student should be using more conventional spelling, and a phonics intervention plan should be created.
d. The student should be encouraged to use a dictionary to confirm spellings of unknown words.

66. Which of the following aspects of reading comprehension belongs in the semantic language domain?

a. Grammar
b. Word order
c. Word meaning
d. Sentence structure

67. What do research studies find about student collaboration relative to effective writing instruction?

a. Cooperative learning does not apply to teaching writing.
b. Cooperative learning is an effective practice for writing.
c. Cooperative learning needs no structure from teachers.
d. Cooperative learning needs structure, not expectations.

68. A sixth-grade student is struggling to comprehend several different types of nonfiction texts. Which strategy would be most likely to assist him with this difficulty?

a. Asking him to reread the text multiple times to locate key information
b. Providing him with a story map to complete while reading
c. Teaching him to recognize the features of different nonfiction text structures
d. Asking him to summarize the main points of each text

69. Students in a sixth-grade classroom are reading a persuasive essay about the importance of recycling. Which question can the teacher ask to help students develop evaluative comprehension skills?

a. Do you agree with the author that recycling is an easy way for everyone to help the environment?
b. Which material takes longer to decompose: plastic or glass?
c. What types of materials can be recycled?
d. Who should you contact in your city if you want to help organize a recycling program?

70. Which instructional activity is the best example of the research-based strategy of activating students' prior knowledge before reading?

a. Before students read a text, the teacher instructs them in relevant background information.
b. Before and after they read a text, the teacher has students make a KWL chart on its subject.
c. After students have read a text, the teacher asks them what they know about the subject.
d. The teacher asks students to express their opinions and reactions on a topic after reading.

71. Which statement best describes the relationship between phonological awareness and phonemic awareness?

a. Phonological awareness and phonemic awareness are interchangeable terms.
b. Phonological awareness is one specific component of phonemic awareness.
c. Phonemic awareness is one specific component of phonological awareness.
d. Phonological awareness typically develops after phonemic awareness.

Refer to the following for question 72:

A class will visit an assisted living facility to interview residents about their lives. Each group of three has selected a theme such as love, work, or personal accomplishment and written several questions around that theme. Next each group practices interviewing one another. The teacher then asks all the students to discuss the questions that caused them to respond most thoughtfully, as well as those they were less inspired by. The students decided the questions that were easiest to respond to were those that asked for very specific information; for example, one inspiring question was, "Please tell me about something you learned to do as a child that affected the direction of your life." Those that were uninspiring were too broad, for example, "Please tell me about your happiest memory."

72. The genre the teacher expects is:

a. Memoir
b. Historical fiction
c. Biography
d. Autobiography

73. Which of the following questions requires students to make an inference about a fictional text?

a. Did the author support her points with strong evidence?
b. How do you think the character felt when she said that?
c. What do you think will happen next?
d. Does this character remind you of any characters in other books you have read?

74. A teacher wants to help her students develop metacognitive skills. Which guiding question can she prompt students to ask themselves while reading?

a. Who are the major and minor characters?
b. Were my predictions correct?
c. What happened first?
d. What is the theme of the story?

75. During a reading assessment, which of the following student behaviors reflects a weakness in strategy?

a. The student tries to read every word, with many errors.
b. The student pays attention to the punctuation in a text.
c. The student understands the main idea, but not details.
d. The student takes a holistic approach to reading words.

Refer to the following for question 76:

A fourth-grade student struggles to decode several words in her science textbook, including *organism*, *conclusion*, and *prediction*.

76. Which text feature could the teacher direct the student to use to best assist with this difficulty?

a. Table of contents
b. Headings
c. Index
d. Glossary

77. Research finds that the challenge of assessing learning in ESL student is best met by which of the following?

a. Written tests
b. Oral assessments
c. Performance assessments
d. (B) and (C) more likely than (A)

78. Which of the following options best describes decodable texts?

a. They contain a predictable text structure that allows emergent readers to guess what will come next.
b. They allow students to apply newly learned phonics skills while reading new texts.
c. They contain a large amount of content-related words to reinforce vocabulary development.
d. They are books with complex plot development that are ideal for close reading analysis.

79. Which of the following activities best demonstrates a multisensory approach to teaching letter formation?

a. Locating words containing a certain letter in a book
b. Tracing prewritten letters on paper with a pencil
c. Identifying letters on flashcards
d. Writing letters in shaving cream

80. When assessing pre-reading skills in typically-developing preschoolers, which of the following skills should NOT be expected?

a. They should be able to recite the full alphabet.
b. They should be able to recite all numbers from 1-10.
c. They should be able to sound out three-lettered words.
d. They should be able to tell whether or not two words rhyme.

81. In a parent-teacher conference to discuss a fourth-grader's progress, both the parents and the teacher agree that they each need to take steps to support the education of the student. Which of the following could the teacher suggest for keeping track of steps being taken at home and at school?

a. Request the parents discuss necessary interventions with their child to make the child more willing to accept the steps being taken to assist him or her.
b. Create a spot in the child's daily folder for parents and teachers to communicate regularly about interventions, progress, and problems that may arise.
c. Hold conferences with the parents once a week to discuss the progress that has been made with the student.
d. Suggest the parents hire a personal tutor for the child to implement the interventions and collect data for the student.

82. "Code knowledge" facilitates reading fluency because:

a. It brings the entirety of the student's previous experience to bear on decoding a text.
b. It offers a framework for organizing new information by assigning code words to sets of ideas.
c. There is no such thing as "code knowledge." The correct term is "core knowledge."
d. It offers a systematic approach to untangling the wide variety of vowel sounds when an unfamiliar word is encountered.

83. Which of the following genres is most important for children just beginning to become readers in grades K, 1, and 2?

a. Alphabet books, wordless picture books, and easy-to-read books
b. Legends and tall tales
c. Biographies and informational books
d. Chapter books and fantasy books

84. Reciprocal teaching activities focus on four main reading strategies. What is the fourth strategy, in addition to summarizing, questioning, and predicting?

a. Evaluating
b. Connecting
c. Retelling
d. Clarifying

85. Which of the following options best demonstrates a kinesthetic activity to build sight word recognition?

a. Circling sight words found in a magazine article
b. Building sight words with letter tiles
c. Reading books containing numerous sight words
d. Hopping along sight words written in chalk

86. A teacher is working with a student who is struggling with reading. The teacher gives him a story with key words missing:

The boy wanted to take the dog for a walk. The boy opened the door. The ____ ran out. The ___ looked for the dog. When he found the dog, he was very ______.

The student is able to fill in the blanks by considering:

a. Syntax. Oftentimes, word order gives enough clues that a reader can predict what happens next.
b. Pretext. By previewing the story, the student can deduce the missing words.
c. Context. By considering the other words in the story, the student can determine the missing words.
d. Sequencing. By putting the ideas in logical order, the student can determine the missing words.

87. After students have studied metaphors for several days, a teacher wants to assess their abilities to apply their knowledge of what a metaphor is. Which assignment would be most appropriate for this purpose?

a. Underlining the metaphors in a sample text
b. Explaining what a metaphor is to a classmate
c. Writing a paragraph that includes at least two metaphors
d. Critiquing the author's use of metaphors in a poem

88. A third-grade teacher is planning a unit in which students will independently read a work of fictional literature. Which of the following prereading strategies would likely be most effective in enhancing students' overall comprehension of the text?

a. Administering a diagnostic exam to determine students' level of literacy development
b. Providing students with a word bank of unfamiliar vocabulary from the text
c. Scaffolding the text by chunking it into smaller parts
d. Having students complete an anticipation guide prior to reading the text

89. What statement is correct regarding effective teacher techniques for classroom discussions?

a. Teachers making comments instead of asking questions encourages creativity in student responses.
b. When some students dominate discussion, teachers engage others with more challenging questions.
c. To meet learning goals, teachers can redirect off-subject discussion by restating topics and questions.
d. A checklist based on the class attendance roll is not the best way to assess all students' participation.

Refer to the following for question 90:

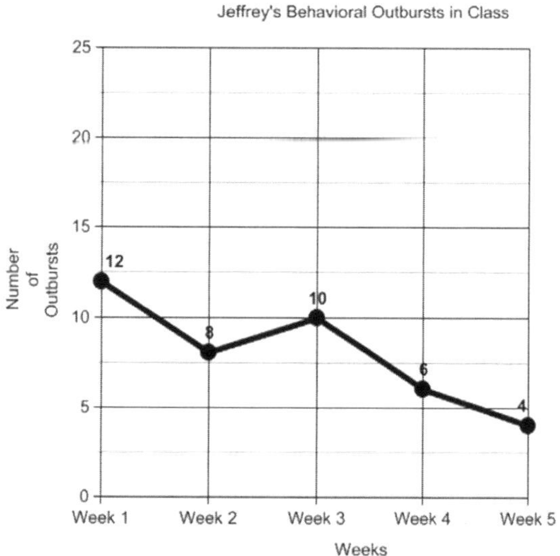

90. This student received an intervention to reduce behavioral outbursts in class. What effect has this had by the fifth week, according to the graph's data?

a. His outbursts have decreased by one-third of what they were.
b. His outbursts have decreased to one-third of what they were.
c. His outbursts have decreased by one-half of what they were.
d. His outbursts have decreased to one-half of what they were.

Answer Key and Explanations for Test #2

1. B: Several researchers studying data from a national sample of teenagers found that high school students not only scored higher on reading achievement tests, but also got higher English grades, when their parents checked their homework (A), discussed school plans with them (B), kept high educational expectations for them (C), and discussed future plans with them (D). The researchers concluded that parental support and interest for reading and other school subjects continues to enhance academic development through the high school years.

2. A: In (A), the teacher guides previewing of information to show students how to put themselves in the right frame of mind to listen carefully for meaning. Students are then able to listen in a guided way based upon the previewing. By varying the type of comprehension assessment, the teacher will get a better understanding of what the students learned. (B) is a good exercise but does not provide for direct instruction by the teacher or a particularly skilled student. In (C), students are focusing more on reading comprehension than listening since they must read the story to themselves and then write a report. There is then no way to gauge what they have learned. (D) would be useful but does not include teacher-guided previewing, which is very helpful in building comprehension.

3. B: Sequencing in language arts is a reading comprehension skill that refers to one's ability to recall and arrange events from a text. If a student struggles with sequencing, the teacher must implement appropriate interventions, as development of this language skill is necessary for success in learning across content areas. For example, sequencing also applies to one's ability to follow a set of directions or steps in the correct order to solve problems; recognize cause and effect; and recall major events from history. In this situation, providing visual aids—such as graphic organizers, story maps, and pictures that correspond with events from stories—supports the student in developing this language skill. The teacher must continuously monitor this student's progress to determine if additional interventions are necessary.

4. D: Phonemic awareness refers to the ability to identify and manipulate sounds at the phoneme level. Because phonemes are the smallest units of spoken sound, phonemic awareness is the most advanced phonological awareness skill.

5. B: Typically, guided practice follows modeling. Independent practice and application would then follow the guided practice, and generalization would come last. Feedback should be provided throughout multiple levels of instruction, particularly during the practice phases.

6. A: Nonsense words refer to those which are spelled and pronounced phonetically but carry no actual meaning in the English language. Incorporating these words into phonics instruction is a beneficial strategy for promoting and evaluating students' ability to decode and blend words with automaticity. Whereas students may sometimes be able to rely upon memory when reading aloud high-frequency sight words, nonsense words prompt students to notice and pronounce each letter sound individually. In doing so, students must distinguish individual phonemes and ultimately blend them together to correctly pronounce the nonsense word. When introducing nonsense words, teachers should begin with monosyllables and increase complexity to multisyllabic words as students develop their blending and decoding skills.

7. B: In order to teach segmentation, i.e., separating linguistic units into their component parts, on multiple phonological levels, the educator must teach students to separate sentences (a higher level) into their component words (A) and to separate words (the next level down) into their component syllables, or into their onsets (initial phonemes) and rimes (following phoneme groups)

(C). They must also teach students to separate syllables into their individual phonemes (D). Whereas choice B includes multiple phonological levels, the other choices only address one phonological level each.

8. D: Decoding depends on an understanding of letter–sound relationships. As soon as a child understands enough letters and their correspondent sounds to read a few words, decoding should be introduced. The act of decoding involves first recognizing the sounds individual letters and letter groups in a word make and then blending the sounds to read the word.

9. A: Among instructional strategies defined by a master teacher (Robb, 2002), asking students open-ended questions about the texts they read is the most useful for helping students to read critically. Teaching students how to skim text for headings, subheadings, boldface, illustrations, captions, sidebars, the index, and other text features that give signs (B) of pertinent material is most useful for helping students locate information. Guiding students to make connections between text and their own personal experiences (D), everyday life (C), world events, and other texts is most useful for helping students understand the relevance of learning materials.

10. C: Close reading involves multiple readings of the same text, with students analyzing different layers of the text each time. Students read the texts independently, with no picture walks or pre-teaching beforehand. Close reading is designed to help students become actively involved in the reading process and develop deeper understandings of what they have read. Guided reading is done in small groups, with teachers focusing on targeted skills based on students' needs. Additionally, picture walks are often done in guided reading groups. SQ3R is a strategy often used to help students comprehend textbook readings. It involves students doing a quick survey of the text, followed by identification of questions about the text. Students then read the text, recite it in their own words, and review the main idea. Scanning involves reading quickly to identify specific information.

11. B: Indirect ways in which students receive instruction and learn vocabulary include through daily conversations, reading on their own, and being read aloud to by adults. Direct instruction and learning in vocabulary include teachers providing extended instruction exposing students repeatedly to vocabulary words in multiple teaching contexts, teachers pre-teaching specific words found in text prior to students reading it, and teachers instructing students over extended time periods and having them actively work with vocabulary words.

12. A: It is important to evaluate specific reading skills, such as phonemic awareness, in a variety of contexts. Reading aloud with Abi allowed his teacher to notice that he consistently misread words beginning with digraphs. Digraphs are sounds in which two distinct letters, when combined, produce a single third sound (e.g., when *s* and *h* produce the *-sh* sound). Blends are words in which two letters produce a third sound which is a combination of both sounds put together (e.g., *b* and *l* combined to make *bl*). The only set of words consisting only of digraphs is choice A.

13. B: Because Elizabeth will be including facts about all stages of Helen Keller's life, as well as how she learned to communicate over time, a time-order, or chronological, text structure is the best fit. Time-order text structures tell the key points about the topic in sequential order. The other options could be used to share information about her life, but they would not be as logical of a fit for this type of biographical report, as they may weave back and forth between different time periods to show relationships between events.

14. B: When using scaffolding, a teacher assigns a task that is just beyond the student's current level. The teacher encourages the student's attempts at comprehension by offering various supports that largely depend on prior knowledge, in order to develop the student's willingness to move forward into uncharted territory as a confident independent learner.

15. D: Denotative meanings are the literal meanings of words found when they are looked up in the dictionary. Connotative meanings are the ideas or feelings evoked by the words. Therefore, two words can have the same denotative meaning in the dictionary, yet evoke very different reactions from readers. *Frugal* and *cheap* can both mean costing little, yet *cheap* often carries a negative connotation. For example, people may be insulted if they were called cheap, yet take pride in being referred to as frugal. The remaining pairs of words have similar meanings, and they all evoke positive feelings.

16. D: Predicting what (like a quest or a war) or whom (such as a prince or three animals) a book is about is a common practice of students who fall back on the easiest answer to a teacher's request to make predictions. It is more useful for teachers to challenge students to try to predict what a character in a novel will do or a significant event that may occur in a story. Teachers can explain to students that they can make predictions by looking for clues in book titles, front-cover illustrations, and illustrations inside a book before even reading it. They can also have students read just one passage from a book, and then have them predict what will occur next.

17. A: Phonics instruction in the early grades has proved most beneficial in developing reading proficiency. Storytelling teaches important speaking and listening skills, but these are different from reading skills. While real literature may increase students' interest in reading, basal texts are well-designed to teach the essential skills.

18. D: When students ask themselves how the information in a text they are reading fits with what they already know, they are relating the text to their own prior knowledge, which increases their reading comprehension. Students should not only ask themselves what kinds of "expert questions" fit the subject matter of the text (A)—e.g., classification, physical, and chemical properties are typical question topics in science; genre, character, plot, and theme are typical of literature questions; sequence, cause-and-effect, and comparison-contrast questions are typical of history—but also what questions the material brings up for them personally (B). It is necessary and important for students to ask themselves continually how each text portion relates to its chapter's main ideas (C) as they read to optimize their reading comprehension and retention.

19. C: Phonemic awareness refers to one's ability to decipher, identify, and manipulate individual sounds within spoken words. Developing this skill in young children is integral to building phonological awareness, which is the ability to differentiate and understand words and sounds within spoken language as a whole. Activities focused on developing students' phonemic awareness, such as rhymes, songs, and alphabet games, emphasize individual sounds within words. Implementing such activities helps establish the foundation of understanding necessary for literacy skill development.

20. B: In the hand outline instructional strategy (cf. Cox, 2009), the thumb (A) represents the topic sentence. This is logical as the hand has only one thumb, and it is a small but important part. The palm (C) represents the main idea, which is logical since it is a single, important, and larger part. The back of the hand (D) is not used, since a two-dimensional drawing would require drawing two hands or turning the paper over. The fingers (B) represent the supporting details, a logical match because there are multiple fingers on a hand and they are smaller than the palm.

21. C: Researchers (Henderson and Mapp, 2002) reviewing the literature found that when middle school and high school students' families remained involved in their educations, they made transitions to new schools better than others (A), maintained their work quality (B), made more realistic plans for the future (C), and were less likely to drop out of school than others (D).

22. C: Long before babies are able to speak, read, or write, they learn language skills by listening. Through listening, children learn rules of grammar, syntax, and pragmatics. They also develop their vocabularies.

23. A: Formative assessments occur continuously throughout instruction to evaluate students' understanding and progress toward reaching academic standards. This style of assessment lets the teacher identify strategies, activities, or approaches that may need adjustment, and incorporate modifications and accommodations to better meet students' learning needs. By reviewing responses to journal prompts focused on opinion writing, the teacher can formatively assess students' mastery of this writing style, and can change instruction as necessary to enhance understanding prior to a formal assessment.

24. A: When readers consider why an author wrote an informational text, determining author purpose gives them greater insight into the text, so choice A is correct. Choice B is incorrect because considering author purpose helps to develop rather than weaken critical reading skills. Choice C is incorrect because considering author purpose helps readers form expectations and engage more thoroughly with the text. Choice D is incorrect because considering purpose helps to engage the reader and allows for a stronger response, making the text more meaningful for the reader.

25. D: The word *maple* begins with an open syllable, spelled *ma*. Open syllables end with a vowel and usually have a long vowel sound. Knowing this will help the student decode this word and other words with open syllables. This word does not contain any vowel digraph pairs, r-controlled vowels, or closed syllables. Vowel digraph pairs consist of two vowels that together make one sound. R-controlled vowels consist of a vowel before the letter *r*. Closed syllables end with a consonant and usually have a short vowel sound.

26. C: Acquisition and comprehension of academic language is a common challenge among young children. Early language development typically occurs in familiar settings, and reflects children's daily interactions and experiences, whereas academic language is content-specific, often more complex in nature, and therefore harder to understand. However, this skill is necessary for literacy development and success in learning across subject areas. In this situation, the teacher implements before-, during-, and after-reading strategies to promote understanding of the academic language students will encounter in the informational text. The teacher contextualizes new vocabulary by providing definitions and examples before students read the text, creating a framework for increased comprehension. By having students complete guided summary frames as they engage with the text, the teacher encourages close reading that promotes students' ability to summarize, and therefore, demonstrate understanding, of what they have read. Additionally, in instructing students to discuss their summaries with a partner, the teacher encourages students to practice using academic language, thus strengthening their comprehension of its meaning.

27. C: Summative assessments typically occur at the end of a lesson or unit to evaluate students' level of progress toward achieving academic standards. These assessments measure students' mastery of particular skills to help inform future instruction and identify the potential need for remediation. In this situation, the teacher wants to see if students have mastered using transitional phrases to organize events in a story. Therefore, instructing students to write an original narrative as a summative assessment would be the most effective approach in evaluating their understanding of this concept.

28. C: This sentence contains the word *firm*, which is an antonym for *tentative*. This antonym, along with the word *unlike*, help the reader determine that *tentative* means not firm. There are no synonyms, or words that mean the same, for *tentative* in the sentence. There are also no definitions for the word. Inference clues give hints about the word's meaning without explicitly listing a synonym, antonym, or definition. No such inference clues are present.

29. C: Research has found the potential of many gifted and high-achieving students wasted when schools do not engage and challenge them sufficiently and appropriately. Studies show that 90 percent of high achievers from all income levels attend college (A); however, low-income high achievers have less likelihood of graduation. Experts advise giving high achievers less directive, more open-ended questions and assignments (B) for greater challenges, and, since abilities vary widely, they also advise letting them collaborate across classrooms and grade levels (C) to find ideal matches. Differentiating instruction is as important for high achievers as struggling students, requiring more support personnel in lower grades (D) where children cannot work independently.

30. B: Aidan is writing to convince the cafeteria manager to act on a specific request, and he supports his request with reasons. This is indicative of persuasive writing. When authors write to inform, they share information about their topics to teach readers new things. When authors write to entertain, they write to provide readers with enjoyable experiences. When authors write to describe, they write to share descriptive details about their topics.

31. C: Choice A is an example of a student reading strategy based on morphology and semantic clues to determine the appropriate prefix. Choice B is an example of using semantic cues to meaning: "horrible" more likely modifies "disaster," "mess," "mistake," etc., than "happiness," "celebration," "opportunity," etc. Choice C is an example of using syntactic cues to meaning: in English, standard word order dictates that adjectives precede nouns. Choice D is an example of decoding difficulties or reading only one word at a time, which interfere with student reading strategies using grammatical, syntactic, or semantic cues to meaning.

32. B: The topics of cooperative projects and/or discussions and whether they are age-appropriate in difficulty relate most to cognitive developmental levels, i.e., what they can understand. Social developmental levels (A) relate to whether students can interact effectively in peer groups. Emotional developmental levels (C) relate to student emotional intelligence, i.e., emotional self-management plus sensitivity to, understanding of, and appropriate response to others' emotions. Behavioral developmental levels (D) relate to whether students can regulate their behaviors appropriately within peer groups.

33. B: In this activity, students are identifying the discriminating phoneme in two words. In the example of *tap* and *top*, it is the middle phoneme that is different. To practice phoneme substitution, the teacher would give students a word and then instruct them to change one of the phonemes and identify the newly formed word. In phoneme deletion, the teacher would give students a word and instruct them to remove a phoneme and identify the newly formed word. In phoneme insertion, the teacher would give students a word and instruct them to add a phoneme and identify the newly formed word.

34. A: The type or pattern of error most damaging to reading proficiency is substituting words with similar appearances or spelling but completely different meanings, because this shows a lack of reading for meaning. Substituting synonyms (B) shows some comprehension of word meaning. Substituting like parts of speech (C) shows some comprehension of grammar and syntax. Substituting correct words or closer approximations for errors based on information from the sentence context (D) shows skills in both reading for meaning and self-correction.

35. A: I-Charts or Inquiry Charts guide students to collect evidence from multiple information sources to support their ideas. While I-Charts are one type of graphic organizer, graphic organizers in general (B) organize and depict information more visually and simply; many do not involve finding or organizing information sources as I-Charts do. Journaling (C) helps students develop their own ideas rather than find or use evidence to support them. RAFT (D), i.e., Reader, Audience, Format, Topic, is a reading or writing strategy that helps students understand those four components' roles, comprehend informational text, and think creatively rather than find and use supporting evidence.

36. B: The alphabetic principle is the understanding that each letter of the alphabet corresponds to a specific sound, and some letters can be grouped with others to produce certain sounds. Understanding the alphabetic principle is necessary for the development of reading and writing skills in young children. To prevent students from feeling overwhelmed and ensure they internalize this concept, it is important to teach and focus lessons on new letters individually or a few at a time. Doing so helps students understand and remember which sounds are produced by each letter or group of letters.

37. B: Receptive and expressive language skills are fundamental to literacy development among young children. Receptive language skills (the ability to understand and internalize language) are necessary for developing expressive language skills (the ability to accurately produce language). Both are necessary for building the background knowledge and vocabulary necessary for effective skill development in all areas of literacy, and therefore must be emphasized in the early childhood classroom. By reading aloud to students and providing explanations and visual examples, the teacher conscientiously promotes receptive language skill development. Further, in asking an open-ended question after the read-aloud, the teacher encourages expressive language skill development by prompting students to use expanded vocabulary to describe their favorite parts of the story.

38. C: The WWC recommends differentiated instruction to students in all three tiers of RTI programs. However, it recommends intensive instruction (A) only for students in Tiers 2 and 3 (20-40 minutes three to five times weekly for Tier 2, daily for Tier 3). Small-group instruction (B) is common to Tiers 2 and 3 to enable more intensive intervention; Tier 1 typically encompasses independent, paired, small-group, and whole-class instruction. While the WWC panel concedes that the ideal primary-grades classroom reading instruction would be evidence-based (D), it finds insufficient research evidence on which to base it.

39. D: Synthesis involves gathering information from multiple sources and combining it to make meaning, as students are doing when they write their research reports on sustainable farming practices. As students collect information from each source, they also consider how their initial thoughts on the topic have changed. Evaluating involves making a judgment about something. Inferring involves using clues in the text to make meaning rather than using information that is directly stated. Drawing conclusions involves making judgements based on inferences.

40. B: Writing haikus will promote students' vocabularies. The tightly controlled syllabic requirements will cause students to search for words outside their normal vocabularies that will fit the rigid framework and still express the writer's intended meanings. Often, students will rediscover a word whose meaning they know, but they don't often use.

41. B: Experts advise teachers not to advance to new letter-sound association material too quickly (A) with students who have recall or naming difficulty, because they need extensive practice or they will forget the associations they were taught before (B). Overlearning is recommended for these students (C). They should perform not only perfectly, but automatically to enable good decoding and encoding. Teachers should not focus only on new material, but combine reviewing earlier instruction with new instruction in every lesson (D).

42. D: Using quotation marks around quotations, and around certain types of titles, is an appropriate goal for students in grades 3-5. Using periods after declarative sentences (A), using question marks after interrogative sentences (B), and using commas to divide series of words (C) are all appropriate benchmarks for students in grades K-2.

43. D: A story map helps students identify the main events of a fictional story, along with the conflict and resolution. Listing the main events can assist Michael with writing a concise summary. A KWL chart helps students identify what they know, want to know, and learned about a topic. A semantic map contains a word or concept in the center of a diagram, with related words or phrases branching off from the middle. It is useful for helping students identify relationships between concepts. A Venn diagram helps students compare and contrast two or more things.

44. D: A device is the best method for helping this student successfully participate in group assignments. Assistive technology can help nonverbal or low-level language students become more independent in the classroom. It can help them form meaningful social interactions in the classroom with other students and can increase their confidence, which will allow them to learn more. Excusing students from group work or pairing them with other nonverbal students does not help the student develop, and may even hold them back from learning new skills.

45. C: Multiple researchers have found that effective programs that promote independent reading by students in school, libraries, and at home share the common elements of access to varied material to appeal to all preferences and age levels, active parental involvement in student reading, collaborations among other significant adults in students' lives, and partnerships among community institutions. It is not just one of these (A) that effective programs commonly share, nor only two (D); and significant adults' collaboration is not more important than active parental involvement (B).

46. A: This example describes the think-pair-share strategy, where a teacher poses a question, gives students time to think about their responses independently, and then puts them in pairs to discuss their responses together. Next, students discuss the responses as a whole class. In the jigsaw approach, students are put into small groups, and each student is assigned one portion of the content that he or she is responsible for learning and presenting to the group. Close reading involves multiple readings of the same text, exploring deeper layers each time. Cloze reading involves giving students a brief passage with some omitted words, which students fill in using clues or background knowledge.

47. C: Word families are an effective strategy for teaching CVCe words. Once students have determined the sound made by the last three letters using knowledge of the silent *e* rule, they can identify other rhyming words within the same family by changing the first letter. This increases the number of words they can easily decode. Because these words have a silent letter that affects the vowel sound, covering parts of the word, chunking, and blending are not as effective.

48. D: Sending home leveled texts ensures that families have access to books in students' instructional reading levels. Providing the books allows students to read immediately and free of charge without requiring any trips to a library or bookstore. Choice A is also helpful, but without providing appropriate books, there is no guarantee that students will have access to reading materials. Notifying parents of which phonics skills the class practiced can also be helpful, but without providing additional information or materials, parents may not know how to best help their children practice these skills. Studying spelling words addresses the words in isolation rather than providing opportunities to read in context and practice decoding, comprehension, and fluency.

49. D: Charlie did not acknowledge any errors, but instead kept reading after each one. Proficient readers recognize when something does not look right, sound right, or make sense, and they try again until they find the correct words. The teacher can prompt Charlie to stop and question himself when he makes errors until he begins recognizing and self-correcting them on his own. Because Charlie's errors both make sense and sound right in the sentences, he is already using both semantic and syntactic cues. The student only omitted one minor word, which did not change the meaning of the sentence.

50. C: The general rule about splitting doubled consonants pertains most to syllabication, i.e., where to divide words up into their component syllables to inform pronunciation and meaning. Structural analysis (A) pertains to dividing words into component parts like prefixes, roots, and suffixes, which may or may not coincide with syllable divisions. Using common spelling patterns (B) pertains to determining meaning and pronunciation in unfamiliar words by comparing their spelling to the same or similar spellings in familiar words. Using morphemes (D) pertains to identifying the smallest meaningful grammatical units in words, e.g., *-ed* verb endings signify past tense.

51. D: Immersing young students in a literate environment is beneficial in demonstrating the application of literacy in daily life, strengthening literacy skill development and promoting academic achievement. Literacy skills are necessary for effective learning across content areas, so these skills must be taught in a variety of contexts in addition to language arts. By incorporating reading, writing, speaking, and listening opportunities into daily lessons, this teacher effectively infuses literacy throughout the curriculum to create a literate environment for students.

52. A: Critiques of final projects (e.g., art projects, research projects, music recitals) are examples of summative assessments because they measure student achievement following instruction. Oral question-and-answer sessions (b) are examples of formative assessments because they can be brief, can be administered often, and can be used to monitor ongoing student progress. Running records (c) keep track of student performance in real time (e.g., oral reading fluency) and are also formative assessments. Pop quizzes (d) are typically short, may be given at any time, and cover the most recent information during instruction; thus, they are also examples of formative assessments.

53. D: Fluent readers are able to read smoothly and comfortably at a steady pace (rate). The more quickly a child reads, the greater the chance of leaving out a word or substituting one word for another (for example, *sink* instead of *shrink*). Fluent readers are able to maintain accuracy without sacrificing rate. Fluent readers also stress important words in a text, group words into rhythmic phrases, and read with intonation (prosody).

54. A: Authors of scientific informational text, such as research study reports, are likely to state the purpose of their research. They are likely to state their interpretations of the evidence or data their study produced. And in any acceptable research report, they will always identify which variables they studied, the population in whom they studied them, the number of the sample size, the conditions of the experiment, and the research methodology used. However, they are least likely to state explicitly their point of view about their research, unlike authors of other types of informational text who directly state their viewpoint about the topic and/or their reason(s) for writing about it.

55. B: This prompt focuses not only on reading fluency skills, but also on the issue of the young reader's confidence. It is very common for students who feel unsuccessful at reading to avoid the skill altogether. The teacher in this question realizes something important: it is vital to build a student's confidence with reading as he or she builds skill. In choice A there is a faulty assumption that a student could ever memorize enough words to eliminate the need to decode. While some students with processing disorders or different learning styles do rely more heavily on sight words, this practice should not be solely relied upon. In choice C the students will likely feel negatively about being asked to read young children's books; their lack of confidence may be reinforced by this plan. In choice D students may also be frustrated by the extra work they are required to do without any evidence of success with this practice. In choice B, students can build their fluency skills by creating words with various sounds, which is often easier for students than decoding as they are learning to read. As their knowledge of letter-sound relationships grows, they will become better at decoding words they see on the page. Allowing students to encode will also provide them with more chances to feel successful as they learn.

56. B: What may seem contradictory actually just includes two aspects: on the one hand, denotative meaning is synonymous with dictionary definition (D); many sources define the former as the latter. On the other hand, dictionaries do not only provide denotative word meanings (A) or only connotative word meanings (C). Many dictionaries provide both denotative and connotative meanings for a word, with examples of each in sentences (B).

57. C: There are many genres from which students can choose to read. The most elemental distinction between genres consists of fiction and non-fiction, the latter referring to stories or texts that are true, or factual. Fictional texts can fall into a variety of categories. Realistic fiction seems as though it could be true. These stories involve realistic characters and settings with which readers can often identify. This type of fiction can consist of different subjects, but it still must be relatable in nature.

58. A: Emergent readers are learning concepts of print, and they benefit from having text in familiar places to assist with tracking and directionality. They are still developing phonics skills and may rely on one or more cueing systems, so picture support is important for determining unknown words. Emergent readers also benefit from simple sentence structure and repetition, which assists them with guessing unknown words. The features in choice B are more appropriate for early readers who are beginning to read more complex texts and are able to use phonics skills and multiple cueing systems rather than relying on picture clues. The features in choice C are more appropriate for transitional readers who are able to read a wider range of genres and text structures independently. Choice D is appropriate for fluent readers who are able to read complex, technical, and abstract texts independently.

59. C: Predicting events in a story builds anticipation and helps propel the reading forward. Students activate prior knowledge from life and literature to understand characters and anticipate their thoughts and actions.

60. B: Based on the research literature, guidelines for phonemic awareness instruction include using analysis of data from phonemic awareness assessments to drive instruction, because only a minority of students requires explicit instruction in phonemic awareness (A). However, effective instruction in phonemic awareness does explicitly label phonemes (C), as well as demonstrates phoneme blending and segmenting processes. Effective phonemic awareness instruction is also differentiated to account for individual differences, including various levels of scaffolding for different students (D).

61. B: Semantic maps are used to create visual representations of connections between items. Students can put the root in the middle of the semantic map and display words containing the root on the branches, thus demonstrating what the words have in common. Looking up words in the dictionary or finding them in the textbook does not facilitate making connections unless follow-up discussions or activities occur. While Venn diagrams are used to compare and contrast two or more things, the web-like format of the semantic map better displays the connections between related words.

62. A: This student needs carefully organized lessons in decoding, sight words, vocabulary, and comprehension at least three to five times a week. These mini-lessons must be extremely clear, with the parts broken down to the lowest common denominator. The more tightly interwoven and systematized the instruction, the better chance this student will have. This type of learner needs, first and foremost, instruction that has been highly organized into a system that will make sense to her. If possible, she should receive private instruction on a daily basis. The instruction needs to focus on decoding, recognizing words, reading with increasing fluency, enhancing vocabulary, and comprehension. She should be working at the Instructional level, or with texts she can read with at least 90% accuracy.

63. A: Teacher "think-alouds" using text the students are reading reflect the explicit instruction component of modeling, i.e., the teacher demonstrates how to use a comprehension strategy. Before modeling, the teacher should use direct explanation (D) to inform students why or how a strategy aids comprehension and when to use it. After modeling, the teacher helps students learn when and how to use the strategy through guided practice (C). Then the teacher helps students practice applying it (B) until they can do so independently.

64. A: A fictional novel is a form of narrative writing that tells a story. In addition to plot and setting, characters are key elements of narrative. In developing characters, authors depict their personality characteristics, mannerisms, behaviors, and interactions with other characters for audiences interested in personalities, motivations, and relationships in stories. A how-to manual is informational writing. The author's purpose is informing how to do something by giving sequential steps, diagrams, and/or descriptions of the order and/or manner in which it should be done, for readers seeking specific instructions in how to complete a process or task. The writer of a persuasive essay has the purpose of convincing readers to agree with a point or argument. The audience is interested in the issue being argued. The writer of an explanatory paper would seek to clarify facts, ideas, or processes for an audience seeking to understand these.

65. B: Phonetic spelling is common at this age, as children write the sounds that they hear. They typically know how to spell a limited number of words conventionally. This is a typical stage of development, and over time, they will begin to spell more words conventionally as more phonics rules and spelling patterns are learned. Asking an adult or using a dictionary to confirm the spellings of all unknown words can slow down and inhibit the writing process. Additionally, as phonetic spelling is typical at this age and the student has spelled some words correctly, it is unlikely that an intervention is needed based solely on this information.

66. C: Semantics primarily refers to word meaning, often with a focus on the individual word, but sometimes including sentence and paragraph context. Any aspect of language that is used to convey meaning can technically considered a semantic property of language. Grammar, word order, and sentence structure are all aspects of syntax.

67. B: Studies show that cooperative learning is an effective practice for teaching many things, including writing (A). Experts recommend that when assigning cooperative writing partners or groups, teachers provide students with both a structure (C), and explicit expectations (D) for both partnership/group and individual performance.

68. C: Understanding text features can help students locate key information in nonfiction texts. Additionally, understanding how different types of nonfiction texts are typically organized provides predictability and structure when reading new texts, which can assist with comprehension. While rereading and summarizing can be effective, asking the student to locate key information without any additional guidance or scaffolding is less likely to be effective. Story maps, which help students identify story elements, are used to assist with comprehending fictional texts.

69. A: Evaluative questions require readers to form opinions or judgements based on the text. Asking if readers agree with something the author stated is an evaluative question. The remaining questions ask students to recall information only.

70. B: A KWL chart allows students to list they **K**now about a subject before they read, what they **W**ant to know or learn about it, and what they have **L**earned about it after reading. This is a good example of a research-based instructional strategy for activating students' prior knowledge. The teacher giving the students background information is the opposite of finding out what they already know. The teacher asking students what they know about the subject after they have read a text is also the opposite of the goal. Activating prior knowledge before reading enables students to build upon what they already know when they begin reading, as successful readers do, versus beginning to read without thinking, as less successful readers do. Similarly, the teacher should ask students their opinions and reactions about a topic before they read, not after, to activate their existing knowledge.

71. C: Phonological awareness and phonemic awareness are distinct terms. Phonological awareness is a broader term that refers to the ability to identify and manipulate sounds in spoken words. Phonemic awareness is one component of phonological awareness involving the ability to identify and manipulate sounds in spoken words at the phoneme level. Because phonemes are the smallest units of speech, phonemic awareness is an advanced component of phonological awareness. It typically develops after simpler skills, like rhyming and blending.

72. C: A biography relates information about part of the life of an individual. An autobiography is a biography about the writer's own life. A memoir is also autobiographical, but focuses on a theme. Historical fiction uses a setting or event based in historical fact as the background for characters and/or action that is invented.

73. B: Inferring requires readers to use clues rather than explicit evidence to determine the author's meaning. Choice B requires students to use the character's statements to infer how he or she felt at the time. Choice A requires students to evaluate the writing. Choice C requires students to make a prediction. Choice D requires students to make a text-to-text connection.

74. B: Metacognition refers to thinking about one's own thinking. Proficient readers use metacognitive skills to self-monitor their own understanding and make corrections when necessary. Making predictions, and then later assessing and revising them if necessary, demonstrates use of metacognitive skills. The other options require students to recall and/or analyze information, but they do not ask students to reflect on their own thinking.

75. D: Making at least the attempt to read every single word, even with many errors (A), is a strategic strength that gives students decoding practice and, even without success every time, enables their potential. Attending to punctuation in text (B) is a strength, since punctuation can significantly affect meaning (e.g., "Let's eat, Grandma" vs. "Let's eat Grandma"). Even without understanding all details, getting the gist of text meaning (C) is also a strength. However, holistic word reading (D) misses plural or verb tense endings and other morphological changes affecting meaning, reflecting a strategic weakness.

76. D: A glossary contains an alphabetized list of important vocabulary words found in a text, along with their meanings. It is similar to a dictionary. It would be the most helpful text feature for a student to use to determine the meanings of the content-related vocabulary words in the text. The table of contents helps the reader identify which pages contain which topics in the text. Headings help the reader determine the main idea of each section of the text. The index is an alphabetized list of topics in the text, along with the page numbers on which they can be found.

77. D: Written tests traditionally used to assess learning in native English-speaking students are typically not as effective with ESL students, as they do not reveal and may even interfere with ESL student demonstration of what they know and have learned. Oral and performance assessments are generally more authentic measures with students learning English.

78. B: Decodable texts use many words containing previously taught phonics skills, allowing readers to practice those skills in context while reading new books. They can be one component found in classrooms that use explicit phonics instruction. Choice A describes predictable books, which rely more on patterns in language rather than phonics skills, to assist readers with decoding. Because most words in decodable texts contain previously learned phonics skills, they do not often have content-related vocabulary words with more complex spelling patterns. Additionally, the focus is on using decodable words rather than on complex plot development, so they may not be appropriate for close reading activities.

79. D: While all of these options can assist students with learning letter formation, writing letters in shaving cream best represents a multisensory approach. It involves movement, touch, and sight.

80. C: When assessing pre-reading skills in typically developing preschoolers, they should be able to demonstrate some benchmarks. Though they are somewhat flexible, most pre-schoolers are able to demonstrate knowledge of the full-alphabet, often in song-form. They are usually able to count from 1 to 10. They are often able to recognize some sight words, though these are not usually tied to phonetic skills at this age. Preschoolers may recognize some words as whole units, but it is unlikely that they will be able to sound out words from their letter components. Preschoolers do usually have a good grasp of similar sounds and can usually distinguish between rhyming word pairs and non-rhyming word pairs.

81. B: Creating a spot for notes in the child's folder or in another easily accessible place is a strong first step to help support the child's educational journey. This allows the teacher and parents to communicate quickly and easily with each other and to have a running list of their communications for documentation purposes. This allows both the teacher and the parent the opportunity to mention their concerns, struggles, or successes with each other while they are continually working to help the child. Asking the parents to discuss the interventions with the child away from the teacher does not help the child know that the teacher is on the child's side and wants to help him or her. The child should know that everyone is working together to help him or her be successful. Holding regular weekly conferences is likely not something that the teacher will have enough time in the day for, which is why it is better to try to find faster communication opportunities when possible while still helping the student. Suggesting that the parents hire a tutor is not a step that the teacher should take before attempting a variety of intervention methods to see if something else would work for the student.

82. D: It offers a systematic approach to untangling the wide variety of vowel sounds when an unfamiliar word is encountered. Code knowledge, also called orthographic tendencies, is a helpful approach to decoding a word when multiple pronunciation possibilities exist. For example, in the words *toe, go, though,* and *low*, the long O sound is written in a variety of ways. A code knowledge approach teaches a reader to first try a short vowel sound. If that doesn't help, the reader should consider the different ways the vowel or vowel groups can be pronounced, based on what he knows about other words.

83. A: Alphabet books, wordless picture books, and easy-to-read books all promote skills important for children beginning to become readers. The other genres are more suitable for older children with well-developed reading skills.

84. D: Reciprocal teaching is an activity in which students gradually take over the role of the teacher in small groups to discuss texts. The students lead discussions focused on four main reading strategies: summarizing, questioning, predicting, and clarifying. The remaining options are also reading strategies, but they are not typically the focus of reciprocal teaching activities.

85. D: When students participate in kinesthetic activities, they are physically engaged in the learning process. These activities involve movement, such as hopping along the sight words written in chalk. While the other activities can also be used to practice sight words and may involve tactile experiences, they involve less movement and physical activity than hopping.

86. C: By considering the other words in the story, the student can determine the missing words. The student is depending on the information supplied by the rest of the story. This information puts the story into context.

87. C: Writing their own examples of metaphors requires students to apply their knowledge. Identifying and underlining metaphors assesses the comprehension level of Bloom's taxonomy, and defining a metaphor assesses the knowledge level. Critiquing the author's use of metaphors assesses the evaluation level.

88. D: Prereading strategies enhance overall student engagement and comprehension. Activities such as anticipation guides serve to provide context, establish purpose for reading, and elicit prior knowledge to strengthen understanding, evoke interest, and make the learning experience meaningful and relevant for students. These guides typically ask students to agree or disagree with a series of statements related to the reading, and to make predictions about the text. This encourages students to actively engage with the text as they determine whether their predictions were correct, or whether their original opinions remained the same during and after reading, which promotes comprehension.

89. C: An effective teacher technique for meeting learning goals in classroom discussions if students get off the subject is to restate the topics and questions they previously stated. Another good redirection technique is to ask new questions about the same topics. To encourage creative and varied student responses, teachers should ask questions instead of making comments, not vice versa. Teachers making comments discourages students from doing the same, whereas asking questions invites them to offer different feedback. When some students dominate the discussion, a technique whereby teachers can engage more reticent students is to ask less challenging questions, not more: less challenging questions can be answered by any student, even unprepared ones. A checklist based on the class attendance roll is a good way to assess whether all students are participating.

90. B: In Week 1, the number of outbursts was 12; in Week 5, it was four. Because four is one-third of 12, the outbursts have decreased to one-third of what they were. They have not decreased by one-third of what they were (A), which would be a decrease of four, i.e., 12 - 4 = 8. If they had decreased by half of what they were, half of 12 is six, so 12 - 6 = 6. If they had decreased to half of what they were, they would also be six in Week 5.